THE
JAGGED WORD
FIELD GUIDE TO
BEING A MAN

THE
JAGGED WORD
FIELD GUIDE TO
BEING A MAN

IRREVERENT OBSERVATIONS FROM THE BACKYARD, BAR, AND PULPIT

WRITTEN AND EDITED BY

SCOTT KEITH
AND PAUL KOCH

The Jagged Word Field Guide to Being a Man: Irreverent Observations from the Backyard, Bar, and Pulpit

Published by:
Jagged Word Books
PO Box 54032
Irvine, CA 92619-4032

Publisher's Cataloging-In-Publication Data
(Prepared by The Donohue Group, Inc.)

Names: Keith, Scott Leonard, author, editor. | Koch, Paul, 1975- author, editor.
Title: The Jagged Word field guide to being a man : irreverent observations from the backyard, bar, and pulpit / written and edited by Scott Keith and Paul Koch.
Description: Irvine, California : Jagged Word Books, an imprint of 1517 the Legacy Project, [2017] | All entries previously published as blog posts on the jaggedword.com website. | Includes bibliographical references.
Identifiers: ISBN 978-1-945978-37-1 (hardcover) | ISBN 1-945978-37-6 (hardcover) | ISBN 978-1-945978-38-8 (softcover) | ISBN 1-945978-38-4 (softcover) | ISBN 978-1-945978-39-5 (ebook) | ISBN 1-945978-39-2 (ebook)
Subjects: LCSH: Christian men–Conduct of life. | Masculinity–Religious aspects–Christianity. | Men–Family relationships–Religious aspects–Christianity. | Male friendship–Religious aspects–Christianity. | LCGFT: Essays.
Classification: LCC BV4528.2 .K45 2017 (print) | LCC BV4528.2 (ebook) | DDC 248.842–dc23

Jagged Word Books is an imprint of New Reformation Publications.

Printed in the United States of America

ABOUT THE AUTHORS AND EDITORS

DR. SCOTT KEITH

Scott Keith is the executive director of 1517 The Legacy Project and Adjunct Professor of Theology at Concordia University Irvine. He is a cohost of the *Thinking Fellows* podcast and a contributor to *The Jagged Word, 1517 The Legacy Project,* and *Christ Hold Fast* blogs. Dr. Keith is the author of *Being Dad: Father as a Picture of God's Grace.* He earned his Ph.D. from Foundation House, Oxford, under the sponsorship of the Graduate Theological Foundation, studying under Dr. James A. Nestingen. Dr. Keith's research focused on the doctrine of good works in the writings of Philip Melanchthon.

PASTOR PAUL KOCH

Rev. Paul Koch is the pastor of Grace Lutheran Church in Ventura, California, where he has been called to hand over the goods—to kill and make alive and recklessly forgive the broken and hurting. He is the editor of *The Jagged Word* and is proud to work beside great friends in this endeavor. It has been his growing conviction that most of the problems currently facing the Christian Church (whether real or imagined) will be fixed not by so-called experts but by the faithful proclamation of the word.

ADDITIONAL CONTRIBUTORS

RICK RITCHIE
Rick Ritchie resides in Southern California and is a graduate of Christ College Irvine and Gordon-Conwell Theological Seminary. He has contributed to the books *Christ the Lord: The Reformation and Lordship Salvation*, *Let Christ Be Christ*, and *Theology and Apologia*.

CALEB KEITH
Caleb Keith holds a BA in theology and classical languages from Concordia University Irvine. He is the producer of the *Thinking Fellows* podcast and a longtime contributor to *The Jagged Word*.

JOSH KEITH
Josh Keith is apprenticing to become a welder and a blacksmith. He is interested not only in working with his hands but also in the life of the mind as expressed by the work of the hands. Keith is an occasional contributor to *The Jagged Word*.

PASTOR ROSS ENGEL
Rev. Ross Engel is the pastor of St. Peter's Lutheran Church in Middleburg, Florida. He is a Scottish Highland Games competitor. He enjoys reading, discussing, and even arguing about theology,

especially if cigars and a pint, or a pipe and some Irish whiskey, are involved in the discussion.

PASTOR BOB HILLER

Rev. Bob Hiller is the pastor of Community Lutheran Church in Escondido, California. Hiller is a lover of all things sports, but "all things sports" are in line behind Denver Broncos football. He is an avid reader, a dedicated beer taster, and a binge watcher of shows on Netflix.

PASTOR JOEL HESS

Rev. Joel Hess is the fortunate pastor at Emmanuel Lutheran Church in Cadillac, Michigan, where God's reality pierces through our illusions by His word, flesh and blood, and gentle waters. He is the author of many half-written projects, a talented musician, and an artist. His contributions to *The Jagged Word* deal with the intersection of theology, culture, and the arts.

CHAPLAIN GRAHAM GLOVER

Rev. Glover is a Lutheran Church—Missouri Synod active-duty US Army chaplain currently stationed at Schofield Barracks, Hawaii. A servant to God and Caesar, Glover is interested in how Lutherans and Roman Catholics ought to understand their relationship five-hundred years after the Reformation and why the American political model is ripe for its own reformation. Always eager to debate theology and politics, Glover isn't afraid to stir the pot and even kick it over when properly motivated.

ABOUT
THE JAGGED WORD

*T*he *Jagged Word* was born out of a general distrust of bureaucracy and an unreasonable desire to make pietists uncomfortable. Other groups that offer insight and commentary on the church and our world seem to default to positions driven by fear that limit our conversation and participation. The academics fear the institutes of higher learning that employ them, driving their honest conversations behind closed doors. Our pastors fear reprisals from the various subgroups with which they've aligned themselves (contemporary, traditional, missional, confessional, etc.); they fear being alone and therefore toe the party line.

In opposition to all of this, *The Jagged Word* focuses on the freedom found in Christ crucified for us. Our concern isn't with toeing the line or satisfying those locked away in the ivory towers. We are only interested in the proclamation of freedom in Christ alone. Whether we are discussing generational distinctions, political positions, or church fellowship matters, the end we drive toward, and from which we are given the strength to begin, is a word that kills and makes alive.

All the authors are given the freedom to write about topics as they see fit. They have been asked to write from a particular starting point or focus on our encounters in this world, but they have never been censored or told to stay in one corner of the box.

Along the way, we have found that we are not alone. We've found that people like you are unsatisfied with tired practices that focus on everything but the actual handing over of the goods. Your participation in this blog, from reading the posts, to sharing them with your friends and family, to commenting and joining the conversation, is making *The Jagged Word* hard to ignore.

Together, we make this whole endeavor something more than just some friends writing a blog to have some fun. Together, we have conversations that matter, conversations that fear always wants to keep silent. We're glad you've joined us, and we hope you'll add your voices to ours.

CONTENTS

PART TWO: WORKING FOR OUR NEIGHBORS

PART THREE: FAMILY

PART FOUR: FRIENDSHIP

PART FIVE: GOOD SMOKE, GOOD DRINK, AND GOOD FELLOWSHIP

INTRODUCTION

Be watchful, stand firm in the faith, act like men, be strong. Let all that you do be done in love.

—1 COR. 16:13-14

T*he Jagged Word* has always been a place that encourages meaningful conversation about what is happening in the church as it intersects with, reacts to, and challenges current cultural trends. The friends that make up *The Jagged Word* and who have written every week for the last few years have found that there are some common topics that tend to come up over and over again. While we certainly see topics of all things church reoccur, such as worship or preaching, we have also noticed that there has been an ongoing discussion about what it means to be a man.

Such writings reflect a longing that is common in our age. There is a sense that what defines a man has been blurred and confused. Without intending to, the authors below have been conducting their own explorations to uncover something we've lost; they are trying to paint a picture of masculinity.

This collection of essays explores masculinity in an unsystematic way. We've found that the various ways we've approached masculinity tend to fall into some broad and practical categories in our writing. To be a man means to be free to be what God has already declared we are in Christ—His saved and redeemed men. A man is free; we are free from sin, death, and the power of the devil. Being free, a man is then honored to work for his neighbor's good, knowing that his closest neighbors are those whom God has placed closest to him in his life—his family. And just as a man speaks to and cares for his own, so also does a man need to be spoken to and cared for at times. He needs the mutual consolation of the brethren, a brotherhood. To put it simply, a man needs good friends. Over and over again, we find praise for fun, the love of good fellowship, good drink, and good smoke.

We might well say that being a man looks like (1) *Freedom*, (2) *Working for Our Neighbors*, (3) *Caring for Family*, (4) *Having Good Friends*, and for fun, (5) enjoying *Good Smoke, Good Drink, and Good Fellowship*.

Admittedly, this may be more of a jagged manhood, but it is the type that we think best describes what we truly long for. In any case, it describes our friends and the other men we have come to respect. And to be sure, much of what we think is wrapped up in a particular theology. We believe that all have sinned and fallen short of the glory of God. That means that all men are sinful and unclean. They sin in thought, word, and deed, and they need a redemption and a Redeemer that is outside of them. All men need Christ.

Thus all men are saved by God's grace alone, through faith in Christ alone, and for the sake of Christ alone. Our salvation is, from beginning to end, to the glory of God alone. None of our works merit anything. All that we add is sin; Christ alone adds all the merit and in turn gets all the glory. We are saved. We are free. We are men standing in the mercy of God because of Christ alone.

Freely, we are privileged to serve our neighbor. When those who are in Christ serve, they do so in love, not from the perspective of fear. However, when those under the curse of the law—who are burdened by death and the power of the devil—serve others, they do so from fear. But the free man's service is out of love. We desire to serve God, yet part of us knows that He does not need our service, and part of us does not know how to serve Him. And then we see those whom God has called to our lives, and we free men see that in working for our neighbor's good, we thus are serving God. We have heard it said that when we stand before the throne, the King will say, "Truly I tell you, whatever you did for one of the least of these brothers and sisters of mine, you did for me" (Matt. 25:40).

Sometimes it's difficult for us to realize that serving our neighbor often means nothing more than moving through the motions of everyday life. We are called to serve our families, those God has placed closest to us, even in our homes. When asked, "What do these good works look like in everyday life?" often the answer is too simple for some. For me, it often looks like the mornings when I stumble out of bed and make coffee before my wife wakes up. It's those all-too-rare occasions when I actually remember to pour her cup first, bring it to her, and hand it to her with a kiss on the cheek, telling her that I love her. It looks like men serving their families in love.

Serving our neighbor often means having good friends who serve us in return. It is important for men to have good male friends. In many ways, the importance of having friends in life is ineffable; it goes beyond the words we can use to describe it. We know that the love we feel toward our friends is a gift from God to men. Unfortunately, it is a gift that many men struggle to find and keep. Having good male friends is part of the vocation of being a man.

Lastly, men like to have fun. Their joy often comes in ways that are hard for women to understand. It often means hitting each other, making fun of each other, and calling each other horrible names. Free men are secure in who they are, confident enough to give and endure the type of fellowship that dances the line between comradery and insult. These "good times" are often aided by good drink and good smoke. The great authors of the past probably knew this better than we do today. How many scenes of male friendship in great literature are pictures of men surrounded by other men in bars or pubs, all enjoying a good pipe? Think of *The Lord of the Rings*. As trivial as such things might seem on the surface, this is not the case. These are some of the most critical times of a man's life!

When men know that they are free in Christ, they also know that they are free to be good neighbors, husbands, fathers, and friends. They are free to have fun enjoying the mutual consolation of their brothers. These free men also know two things. First, they will fail because they remain sinner-saints. Second, they know that when they fail, they are free to flee to the cross of Christ, who has already covered all their failures.

Be the men you were called to be. You are free men who are freely providing service to neighbors, loving family, and enjoying God's good gifts. Most of all, remember: "If the Son sets you free, you will be free indeed" (John 8:36).

This book is not a systematic exploration of what it means to be a man or how to better live as a man today. It's not a how-to book or some sort of twelve-step guide promising you'll lose inches off your waist or grow more facial hair. We are not life coaches. Rather, what you are holding in your hands is a collection of some of the writings from *The Jagged Word* over the past four years that have highlighted the topic of being a man in one way or another.

To help you join us in this conversation, we've grouped these musings into the five categories referenced above:

1. Free to Be a Man
2. Working for Our Neighbors
3. Family
4. Friendship
5. Good Smoke, Good Drink, and Good Fellowship

The beauty of this is that you don't have to read it from cover to cover, from beginning to end. Each article is independent of the next, so you can read around as you wish. Leave it on the back of the toilet or proudly display it on the coffee table. Read a few while waiting at the dentist or digest the whole book on a long flight.

This collection of articles is our attempt to have you join us in this meaningful discussion. Pick a topic or a title and dive in. Of course, you can always interact with us at thejaggedword.com. And who knows, over time you may very well notice some inches off your waist and your beard coming in a little thicker, but that will probably just be a coincidence.

PART ONE
FREE TO BE A MAN

THE LOST ART OF MASCULINITY

SCOTT KEITH

Have you ever met a man that could change a room by entering into it? I've met a few of them in my time. My mentor Dr. Rod Rosenbladt is one of them. My doctor father, Jim Nestingen, and friend Paul Koch are others. Have you ever wondered what it is about a man that can cause him to have such an effect simply by entering a room? It's masculinity. Being masculine is laudable, not deplorable, though watching TV, going to the movies, and engaging in modern culture don't seem to show us this. Rather, almost every male character portrayed in modern media seems to be stupid, incapable, or irrelevant.

Something has been lost along the path of the moral enlightenment/political correctness that has overtaken our modern culture. Among other things, we've lost the truth that we, our society and culture, need men to be men. We need men to be masculine. Clearly, we do not need men who are abusive, overbearing, or stagnant examples of male domination and chauvinism. Clearly, we could do without those who think that women are lesser by design and unworthy of our respect, dignity, or care. But clearly, we lost something when we stood by and allowed the pendulum to swing so far to the other side, causing men to

be feminized and confused, turning them into examples of inse-
curity and uselessness.

It seems easy to identify what it means to be masculine. To be
masculine is, first, something quiet. Those who are masculine are
not mean or loud, and they will never be perceived as blowhards.
Rather, they are almost unassuming in their demeanor. In turn,
they are not moralists, per se. Sure, they know what is right and
what is wrong, and they will stand up for the right and fight the
wrong. Their sense of right and wrong doesn't lead them to sanctimony and self-righteousness. Rather, their sense of right and
wrong will often lead to forgiveness. Masculine men are capable,
strong, and confident.

And when they can't do something, they are confident
enough to ask a brother for help. In turn, masculine men have
a true sense of *philia*, brotherly camaraderie and love. They will
find other masculine men to surround themselves with, men
whom they can trust. Often, it may seem that masculine
men run in herds because they are always together. This is not
some sort of negative gang mentality. Rather, it is iron sharpening iron. Think of *Tombstone*, *Braveheart*, or *Band of Brothers*.
Men need mutual support to teach them to be men, especially
in our day.

But none of these characteristics enable a man to change a
room by entering it. So then, what is it? It is the sense of grace
that a masculine man brings with him. His unassuming, strong,
confident, capable, humble, and forgiving character seems to
pour forth from his pores like sweat on a hot day. He is strong,
but his strength is not used to abuse. Rather, a masculine
man's strength is used to protect and save. He is confident. But
his confidence is not used to demoralize. Rather, a masculine
man's confidence is shared so that others' confidence in him
becomes his confidence. He is capable. But his capability is used
to build up the weak and destroy the strong and oppressive.
He is not a moralist. Rather, he forgives, confidently, capably,
and unassumingly. A masculine man can forgive as much with

a gesture as with his words. In short, as my friend and mentor Dr. Rod Rosenbladt would say, a masculine man "is a foggy, or out of focus picture of what God is like." Essentially, he is grace and freedom to those he encounters. To be masculine is laudable, not deplorable, and it's a lost art that we ought to rediscover.

LIVE AS THE MEN YOU ARE CALLED TO BE

SCOTT KEITH

God calls men to love. The apostle Paul is clear about this in 1 Corinthians when he claims that, no matter what we say, if we speak without love, we are no better than a banging gong:

If I speak in the tongues of men and of angels, but have not love, I am only a resounding gong or a clanging cymbal. If I have the gift of prophecy and can fathom all mysteries and all knowledge, and if I have a faith that can move mountains, but have not love, I am nothing. If I give all I possess to the poor and surrender my body to be burned, but have not love, I gain nothing. Love is patient, love is kind. It does not envy, it does not boast, it is not proud. It is not rude, it is not self-seeking, it is not easily angered, it keeps no record of wrongs. Love does not delight in evil but rejoices with the truth. It always protects, always trusts, always hopes, always perseveres. Love never fails. But where there are prophecies, they will cease; where there are tongues, they will be stilled; where there is knowledge, it will pass away. For we know in part and we prophesy in part, but when perfection comes, the imperfect disappears. When I was a child, I talked like a child, I thought like a child, I reasoned like a child. When I became a man, I put childish ways behind me. Now we see but a poor reflection as in a mirror; then we shall see face to face. Now I know in part; then I shall know fully, even as I am fully known. And now these three remain: faith, hope and love. But the greatest of these is love. (1 Cor. 13:1–13)

In a sense, how your father treated you when you were growing up doesn't matter. It doesn't even matter if you had a father, because what truly matters is who you are. You are a free child of God who has been called to faith and to freedom in Christ. It is that freedom that allows us to truly love. Paul can say what he does in 1 Corinthians 13:1–13 because he is not talking to those who are yet slaves to the law and the death it brings. Christ is the end of the law for us. We are freed. Having been liberated, we are now free to be servants to one another in love. Love's origin is freedom, which is why love is the greatest. In turn, we are free to forgive.

Some will criticize the idea that the father has a particular role in life, the family, and the home because what is presented here may seem like some kind of backward, antiquated social order. Yet, God's word shows that He tends to work through these social orders how and why He chooses. Vocationally, the role of the father will always be different from that of the mother. We may choose to deny this reality, but our denial does not equate to changing the way things are.

The whole of scripture speaks against a denial of this order. The father is to speak in encouragement and love to exhort his family in the love of the Lord: "For you know how, like a father with his children, we exhorted each one of you and encouraged you and charged you to walk in a manner worthy of God, who calls you into his own kingdom and glory" (1 Thess. 2:11–12). Further, he is the head of the house: "For the husband is the head of the wife even as Christ is the head of the church, his body, and is himself its Savior" (Eph. 5:23). But his headship is intended to point to love, forgiveness, and encouragement. It is not a headship that lords power over those whom he is called to serve. It is a headship meant to be an *analogia entis*, analogy of being, to a good and gracious God.

In *God at Work*, Gene Veith describes the reality that Christians do not give up the natural order of our earthly vocations. Rather, we embrace them in freedom and love. Veith explains, "When He says to live as you were called, he is saying, among other things, do not change your various vocations just because you became a Christian." Instead, understand that God's order, his first use of the law, is still in place among Christians.

We ought to acknowledge that some things we do as men—rightly and wrongly—support our vocations as father, while others detract from it. When we use our power to serve only as a means of punishment and intimidation, we detract from our intended headship and fatherhood. When we disrespect our calling as husbands to our wives, we teach our children that our grace has limits. When we fail to love, we show that we misunderstand what it takes for God to love us—namely, the atonement wrought by His Own Son. But the gospel changes all this. The gospel breaks in and speaks peace, hope, deliverance, forgiveness, and love into our hearts. And on that powerful word of life, we ride into the lives of our families speaking those same words of peace, hope, deliverance, forgiveness, and love. When we do this, our headship in the family is confirmed. When we do this, we teach our children that God's grace has no limits because it took a limitless grace to forgive us. When we act in love, we merely shadow God's love as a pale reflection. But sometimes that pale reflection is just what is needed to provide hope.

The real-life application seems to be that, as fathers, we need to accept our vocations as gifted to us by God. This means that we should be confident in being fathers, not desiring to be something we are not but recognizing our fatherhood as a gift from God. My intent is to show you the importance of your vocation as a dad. Being a dad is a calling so great that it points your children in a real and substantial way to the cross of Christ and a gracious God who loves them and desires them as His children.

My only words of intentionally practical advice to you will be this: You are forgiven in Christ. He has called you to Himself and to be a dad. Be confident in God's purpose for you as a father. As a father, you can be an "analogy of being" to a good God. God has called you to this, and you are merely walking in the steps that He has laid out for you. Live freely as the dad God has called you to be.

YOUR GIRLFRIEND
IS STRONGER
THAN YOU ARE

SCOTT KEITH

My good friend David Rufner sent me an article that riled me up, though it wasn't surprising. Written by David French, the article was in the *National Review* and titled "Young American males are losing touch with a critical element of true masculinity" (French, "Male Physical Decline"). What grabbed me were the first few lines of the article. French says, "If you're the average Millennial male, your dad is stronger than you are. In fact, you may not be stronger than the average Millennial female."

The article recounted a study that analyzed the grip strength of a representation of university-aged guys, noting that their grip strength had decreased significantly between 1985 and 2016. In fact, their grip strength had weakened from 117 pounds of force to ninety-eight. Again, he noted that the young men's grip strength now rivaled that of older millennial women. Mr. French says, "In other words, the average college male had no more hand strength than a thirty-year-old mom."

I knew things were bad, but really? The average millennial male can't beat his girlfriend in a contest of strength? What the hell is going on here? I think this is happening because boys are not taught to succeed in becoming men, at least not real men. We are working on three generations of kids raised almost exclusively by women, compounded by a society that is increasingly feminized, resulting in a distinct lack of masculinity among grown men. Safety has become the paramount goal, even among boys and men, and the type of hard work that turns a boy into a man is scorned.

Most boys today will never learn to change the oil in their car. Why would they when a "quickie" oil change is only $19.95? Further, when was the last time you saw an eleven-year-old mowing a lawn or helping his dad paint a fence? In the not-too-distant past, these were the types of everyday tasks that taught boys that manual labor was not beneath them and that taking care of the home was an integral part of the vocation of being a grown man, husband, and dad.

This reminds me of when my son and I sparred in our front yard. He has taken some boxing lessons, and I like to hit the heavy bag in the garage. So, we thought, why not? We gloved up and went at it. I got a few good shots in, and he rang my bell more than once. The first time he walloped me in the head and "rang my bell," I said, "This reminds me of high school." I was in more than a few fights in high school, and the event took me back in time.

Everybody who watched me get my ass kicked confusedly laughed. Why did they laugh? Well, because such a thing as getting walloped by another boy in high school is a nearly unheard of event. The schoolyard *scrap* is verboten! As Mr. French says in his article, "In the age of zero-tolerance school-disciplinary policies—where any kind of physical confrontation is treated like a human-rights violation—they have less opportunity to develop toughness."

If this has gone on for three generations, and I think it has, then the truth is that a good number of young boys today haven't seen strong masculine men as fathers or mentors that they want to emulate. If young men don't grow up respecting older men, it follows that they also won't grow up wanting to be strong men. Why would any young man want to put in the hard work to become a strong, masculine man? They can't aspire to be a picture of something they have never seen. Young men imagine being a real man as just another grown-up duty like changing the oil or unclogging a toilet, tasks they have never had to do and don't want to do. There is no magic, no wonder, and no greatness for them in doing the types of chores that defined a man's place in the home in the past. So they become more feminine; they become weak as women now learn to be strong.

Our culture has taken vocational integrity from young men just so it can inquire as to why they can't stand on their own two feet. It questions why boys struggle in school. It queries as to why young men seem so useless in the workplace, the whole time refusing to acknowledge that the modern workplace is a distinctly feminine kingdom. At the same time, our culture tends to desire that men be weak while beguiling the results of that weakness.

In his article, Mr. French ends by claiming, "Men were meant to be strong. Yet we excuse and enable their weakness. It's but one marker of cultural decay, but it's telling. There is no virtue in physical decline." I think he is right, and I believe that the implications, especially to fatherhood, are staggering.

Where do we go from here? We need to set our boys free to become men. We need to begin desiring strength over weakness, competence over dependence, and masculinity over passivity. In *Being Dad*, I suggest that "Men need to know that they are free to be what God has created and called them to be: confident, gracious, forgiving, masculine men who are analogies of God to those who don't seem to see Him anywhere else." I said that then, and I think more needs to be said.

WHAT KIND OF MAN ARE YOU?

SCOTT KEITH

I ask myself this question all the time. I'm truly interested in knowing what kind of man I am and how others might answer that question. Perhaps it's narcissistic of me to wonder such a thing. Maybe I ask myself such a question because I more frequently ask it of others. Often, I find answers in the most unexpected places.

Recently, I've been reading *Norwegian Wood: Chopping, Stacking, and Drying Wood the Scandinavian Way* by Lars Mytting. I am an eclectic reader and can often be found reading books on many different subjects. I was hoping this book could give me some insight into preparing next year's full wood supply for our mountain cabin. Imagine my surprise when this wonderful little book, concerned mostly with organizing one's wood stack, turned and helped me answer my preeminent question: What kind of man are you?

Apparently, back when women in the United States wanted to get married and find husbands, those who lived in heavily wooded portions of our country, like Maine, used wood piles to help them discern what kind of man they were courting. Folksy wisdom from the time suggested that a man's wood pile said a lot about him. For those women looking to get married, Mytting provided the following list to serve as a sort of rule of thumb:

- **Upright and solid pile:** Upright and solid man
- **Low pile:** Cautious man, could be shy or weak
- **Tall pile:** Big ambitions, but watch out for staggering and collapse
- **Unusual shape:** Freethinking, open spirit, again, the construction may be weak
- **Flamboyant pile, widely visible:** Extroverted, but possibly a bluffer
- **A lot of wood:** A man of foresight, loyal
- **Not much wood:** A life lived from hand to mouth
- **Logs from big trees:** Has a big appetite for life, but can be rash and extravagant
- **Pedantic pile:** Perfectionist, may be introverted
- **Collapsed pile:** Weak will, poor judgment of priorities
- **Unfinished pile, some logs lying on the ground:** Unstable, lazy, prone to drunkenness
- **Everything in a pile on the ground:** Ignorance, decadence, laziness, drunkenness, possibly all of these
- **Old and new wood together:** Be suspicious, might be stolen wood added to his own
- **Large and small logs piled together:** Frugal, kindling sneaked in among the logs suggests a considerate man
- **Rough, gnarled logs, hard to chop:** Persistent and strong willed, or else bowed down by his burdens
- **No woodpile:** No husband (Mytting, *Norwegian Wood*, 116)

It's been so long since I needed a woodpile that I don't remember what my woodpile says about me. (My past home in Nevada was heated with two pellet stoves, whereas one barely needs a heater in SoCal.). I'll let you know this spring. But this did get me thinking. What does what we produce today say about the kind of men we are? The problem in answering this question is that, for the most part, we produce nothing. Well, let me correct that. Most of us, myself included, produce banter of one type or another.

Blogs and social media provide the opportunity for all of us to produce something. We produce carefully crafted images of ourselves. Perhaps we are more aware than the wood stacker that what we produce tells the world about us. The wood stacker's job has a dual purpose. He stacks wood in a manner that will allow it to dry so that it can be easily burned in the stove during the winter and does so in a manner that reflects who he is. What we produce, however, often maintains only one purpose: to tell the world about us—our sense of humor, thoughts, wit, and wisdom.

So I return to the question. What does what I produce tell the world about what kind of man I am? This is not a question that I can answer for myself. But it might be worth some self-reflection nonetheless. I often worry that we all have been acculturated to a world that despises true masculinity. That we have forgotten not only what it means to be a man but also that how we stack our woodpile says a lot about what kind of man we are.

In *Being Dad: Father as a Picture of God's Grace*, I tried to give a description of masculinity that could serve as sort of a "Woodpile Rule of Thumb." I define masculinity as a male's quiet confidence and strength of character that finds expression in graciousness. It is quiet, firm, strong, and forgivingly gracious and kind. Lastly, masculine men know that they need to be forgiven as often as they need to forgive.

So what do we produce? Is what we produce upright and solid, or is it rough, gnarled, and falling down? Do we have much of value to say or not much at all? Are we flamboyant or collapsed? Is our work unfinished and not well thought out? Are we mean, incredulous, and overly critical? Or do we, as Luther once said, try to put the best construction on everything?

It is tempting to forget that we tell people about who we are by what we produce, even when it comes to our woodpile. When we are strong, people can see that. When we are kind, they see that too. When we act on the behalf of righteousness, they know that. When we are self-serving, they know that. If we are wrong, they can tell, just as they can tell when we are right. They respect when we seek forgiveness and cringe when we are overly arrogant. When condemnation is all we produce, they come to expect that we will eventually condemn them as well. Yet when the forgiveness that we have received in Christ is foremost on our lips, they hear that most of all. When this is the case, all can see that our woodpile is upright and tall because its foundation is solid and unshakable.

Just as our woodpiles say a lot about what kind of man we are, the words and messages we produce do the same. We ought to measure our words in accordance with who we are as men—men standing in Christ alone. After all, you never know, there may be some fine, fine, lady out there examining your woodpile to evaluate whether you might make a good husband. What do you want them to see?

A WASTED LIFE?

SCOTT KEITH

My friend Aaron introduced me to a website that has shattered my world. No, it's not a site spouting a new theology. It's not even promoting a new worldview or philosophy that has got my head spinning. Rather, it is a site dedicated to tools. Yes, tools. The site is John Neeman Tools, and they have a rather simple philosophy. All their tools are made in their small, traditional workshops in Latvia using equally traditional methods and techniques. Their focus is on uniqueness and quality, not quantity. They want to help people remember how to use their hands, how to relate their own human energy to their tools and achieve the true joy of creating something from humble beginnings.

The part of the site that got to me was a simple twenty-minute video called "The Wooden House Project." Again, the stated goal seemed rather simple. Jacob, a carpenter, said that he wanted to build a simple home using local materials such as wood, stone, old and new clay bricks, moss, linen fiber, clay, water, lime, wheat flour, salt, and wood shavings. And that he did. The timbers were hand-cut from logs felled by hand in January, because trees sleep during winter and the moisture content is very low in them then. As time passes, timber felled in winter becomes light and strong.

The video was simply amazing. I had spent a fairly manly weekend hauling cabinets and supplies to our cabin using snowshoes

because the road was not passable, being covered in over four feet
of snow. But this video made every accomplishment in my life
seem small. I felt like less of a man. When I shared the video with
my buddy Dave Rufner, his words sort of summed up my emotions when he replied, "That home building video could make a
man weep. Literally." That it did.

Suddenly, I felt as though I had led a wasted life. Why hadn't
I done something like this? Why hadn't I learned to work with
my hands more proficiently, enough to live sustainably in the
woods somewhere with my wife and kids? Why hadn't I followed
my heart and my dreams and set out to the great unknown and
made a living making things with my own two hands?

And then, lying in my bed at 4:00 am while contemplating
my missed opportunities, it hit me. Life is just life, no matter
where you are or what you're doing. Jacob had obviously left out
many scenes. I never saw him hit his fingers with a hammer, but
he must have. There were almost constant pictures of his kids
running around, but I never saw them get in trouble for mess-
ing up his tools or being where they were told not to be. I never
saw his wife get inordinately pissed off that he was spending too
much time with the other woman: "The Wooden House." In fact,
I never saw one negative thing cross my eyes, just sunshine and
rainbows.

I had another realization. I had done something I liked with
my life. In fact, I have followed my heart on many an occasion.
First, I married my beautiful wife, Joy. Together, we have raised
three wonderful kids. To make a living for my family, I have
worked with my hands and with my mind, sometimes at the
same time. And unlike "The Wooden House Project," the video
of my life that I play in my head shows not only sunshine and
rainbows but also, at times, depression and despair. My life has
been a mix of joy, happiness, repentance, and forgiveness. Praise
be to God!

My life has been and will continue to be what God has intended
it to be. He has called me out of darkness into His marvelous

light. By my baptism and by the proclaimed word in my ears, He has made me His own. He has declared me to be His! And now I live, sinner and saint, walking through the motions of my everyday, somewhat normal life, trying to be what He has already declared I am. A sinful man such as me can do nothing else and hope for nothing else on this side of glory.

I want my life to matter. I do not want my life to be a wasted life. Perhaps this is folly, but perhaps this means that engaging my vocations in ways that are meaningful to me and others is, before the Lord takes us home, part of my purpose here. I want to do good works, and yes, like Paul says in Romans 7, I often fail. But more than that, I think that our common idea of good works is ill-defined.

I do many speaking gigs for the book *Being Dad: Father as a Picture of God's Grace*. Some time ago, when teaching on fatherhood, I realized that the whole work is an argument for taking the vocation of father and the concept of vocation as a whole seriously. In *A More Radical Gospel*, Gerhard Forde wrote:

> *People who complain that Luther has no proper doctrine of good works and sanctification or ethics always seem to forget this understanding of the Christian's calling. Perhaps because it is so utterly realistic and unromantic. But virtually everything Luther wants to say about ethics comes back to his doctrine of vocation. One is to serve God in one's occupation, in one's concrete daily life and its duties in the world. When I tell students that this first of all means that they should pay attention to being better students, they are often a little disappointed. They had more romantic things in mind . . . It does not occur to them that their first ethical duty is to be good students! Whatever call there might be for more extreme action, it must be remembered that Luther's idea is that first and foremost one serves God by taking care of his creation.*

This is an argument for taking vocations seriously. Our first ethical duty is to try to fulfill our vocations to the best of our abilities, whatever they may be. First and foremost, we serve God by taking care of His creation—our family. We serve our closest neighbors and our families through the seemingly mundane motions of everyday life. God's words of life come to our families from the lips of another and, by God's grace, from our lips. As a man and a father, if I have done this even a little, praise be to God, and God forgive me for my abundant failures.

A wasted life? I'm not sure. But what I am now sure of is that if my life is wasted, it is not because I haven't hand-built a timber-framed house. I stand in the one who has redeemed me with His own blood. Because of Him, my Heavenly Father has declared me not a waste, and His declarations always come to fruition. By His word, the entire universe was created; by His word, He saves me and calls me to be what He has already declared I am. I am a saved child of my Heavenly Father—a man, husband, father, author, teacher, director, and even occasional carpenter. Praise be to God in Christ Jesus our Lord, who saves and calls a sinner like me to a life not wasted in Him.

WE ARE NOT DESCENDED FROM FEARFUL MEN

SCOTT KEITH

"**W**e will not be driven by fear into an age of unreason, if we dig deep into our own history and our doctrine and remember that we are not descended from fearful men, not men who feared to write, to speak, to associate, and to defend causes which were for the moment unpopular" (Murrow and Friendly, *See It Now*). These are the words spoken by Edward R. Murrow as encouragement to those who would stand up in opposition to then Senator McCarthy's hearings designed to root out all dissenters, whether they were guilty of being communists or not. Mr. Murrow goes on to remind us all of a simple yet exceptionally difficult reality: "We can deny our heritage and our history, but we cannot escape responsibility for the result."

Of all the current mind-sets that bind our modern cultural milieu, I think it is fear that paralyzes us the most. Fear seems to rule us. Men are afraid to act like men, and women feel they need to degrade others to elevate themselves. Courage of one's convictions is touted as intolerance, and dissent from the current set of acceptable beliefs is a call to violence. Fear guides our motives. Fear of failure or even reprisal guides our actions and our speech. We are afraid to confess our faith out of the fear that our confession will be perceived as too inclusive or not pure enough.

The screaming messages of doom are almost always in our ears telling us to be afraid. Our cars scream at us if we do not fasten our seatbelts quickly enough. Protestors scream at us on TV telling us to be afraid of Donald Trump. Hell, these days, we're even scared to let our kids play outside until the street lights come on because we're told to be fearful for their safety if we let them play in the world.

The bottom line is that we seem to be scared all the time. Yet our national history as well as our theological history (if you are part of a Reformation tradition) tell us that we are not descended from fearful men. Our national history is full of tales of men that preferred death—our ultimate fear—to an imposition on their liberty. Men such as Patrick Henry exclaimed, "Give me liberty or give me death" as a battle cry for the men of his age.

Our theological history is full of tales of bravery and of men who stood for something even in the face of seemingly certain death. Martin Luther famously cried, "Unless I am convinced by Scripture and plain reason—I do not accept the authority of the popes and councils, for they have contradicted each other—my conscience is captive to the Word of God. I cannot and I will not recant anything, for to go against conscience is neither right nor safe. God help me. Amen" ("Luther at the Imperial Diet of Worms"). And though it is now thought to be an apocryphal attribution, the phrase, "Here I stand, I can do no other" rings like fine music in man's ear.

These men stood for something, not just against something or someone. It is our various stands "against" this or that that motivate our current fearfulness. We have damn near lost the ability to stand for something. When we stand up like men and stand for something, though we may be afraid, fear is not allowed to gain a firm foothold because it is not what motivates our stand.

Arguments against almost always need to employ fear as evidence for why the argument has merit. Don't let your kids have too much independence because they might get hurt or make the wrong choices. Don't allow honest and vigorous political or theological conversation because those arguing for the other side might convince some of the "wrong" position. Don't stand for your beliefs, especially if they don't line up with current political or theological morals because you might reveal yourself to be intolerant or heterodox. Fear drives our decisions, and fear is winning.

Freedom is the only answer to a world bound by fear. Freedom and liberty are not the same thing, but they hold some of the same power. Both imply that the holder—of liberty or freedom—is in some way exempt from external control, coercion, interference, restraint, or regulation. One who is free is at liberty to determine how to act without restraint. This is what terrifies fearmongers and law dogs alike.

Freedom is what terrified the British aristocracy in the age of revolution and the papacy in the age of Luther. Our political forefathers were men who proclaimed that they stood for a man's God-given natural right to life, liberty, and the pursuit of happiness. They stood for liberty and freedom in opposition to fear and slavery.

Our theological forefathers stood for something even greater. They believed that the gospel of Christ sets sinners free from sin, death, and the power of the devil. If Christ has done all these things, if God has declared us righteous in Christ, called us to Himself, and set us free, why are we still afraid? Remember: "Neither height nor depth, nor anything else in all creation, will be able to separate us from the love of God that is in Christ Jesus our Lord" (Rom. 8:39). If we are in His hands, we have nothing to fear. Death no longer holds us, nor does the law have the power to condemn us. Christ has set you free, and in Him you are free indeed.

Being free, you no longer need to live a life of fear. Stand for your convictions. Live the life God has called you to live, as brave men who live in Christ, serving your neighbors—freely. Be bold, and speak with love and confidence, not scare tactics. Cling to the liberty that only a free man can know. Let those around you explore their freedom. If we maintain the courage of our convictions, we will not be afraid of other beliefs or views. Rather, we will have the courage to face them, honestly debate them, and stand tall knowing we have stood by the truth, come what may.

Lastly, please remember, we are not descended from fearful men.

THE MASCULINE SPIRIT

PAUL KOCH

While I much prefer my neighborhood Ace Hardware store to the Lowes across town, there is something that makes the trip to Lowes worthwhile. It's not so much the personal shopping experience. I'll take the knowledge of the guys and gals at Ace over Lowes any day. Plus, they have free popcorn! Rather, it's the spectacle found at Lowes that makes it a joy to go there. I've noticed something delightful in the wide and spacious aisles of Lowes. Whether I'm in the plumbing aisle or lumber section, there are often one or two complete novices deep in thought about the correct purchase. And by novices, I mean folks who have absolutely no idea what they're doing. Yet here they are buying PVC cement or a stack of two-by-fours and a box of nails. They're getting ready to give it a try, dirty their hands, and risk screwing it all up, and I think it's a beautiful sight.

Sure, some people may find joy in watching people greet old friends at the airport. They may get all misty-eyed at a wedding, but for me, I love to see the pasty-faced neophyte getting ready to build something for the first time.

There is something about this activity that is inextricably linked to manliness. To engage in a world outside of our own minds, to create with our hands, build, fail and try again, is part of what makes a man. It's not about being the most skilled craftsman or doing what others cannot; it's about trying. There is an incredible spirit of masculinity that is willing to go down swinging while fighting the fear of the unknown. It's not that a bookshelf built by one's own hands will be of higher quality or more durable than the one you pick up at Target (though you might be surprised). Rather, it's the desire to try to build a bookshelf, the movement from an idea to a physical creation, that shapes a man.

Yet there has been a constant and relentless attack on just such a thing. More and more of our lives are defined by experts who are the custodians of the outside world or by technologies that keep us in our heads. In fact, these two things work in concert to provide us with products that leave us, and any tinkering we might be inclined to do, completely outside the loop. We can buy a new car that talks with an app on our smartphone to inform us of what maintenance needs to be done. It will even lead us to the nearest expert to perform such maintenance. Even if we wanted to pull away from the screen long enough to give it a try ourselves, we would find layer upon layer of technological advancements that prohibit us from being able to do much more than stand there and stare inquisitively at a mess of hoses and wires.

In most aspects of life, we are reduced to being consumers. We don't know how things work, and we don't even care. We just want them to work for us. And if they don't, we take them to an expert. We are increasingly encouraged to stay within our own minds and only tamper with things if we happen to be an expert in that field. Otherwise, we just leave it to the carpenter, plumber, mechanic, theologian, or psychologist.

I think this leads us to a sad state of affairs. It leads us to a place where men fill their days doing some of the most bizarre shit imaginable because they have lost the spirit of masculinity and are reduced to nothing more than collectors and critics.

This became increasingly clear last Christmas day. After all the gifts were unwrapped, church, and a wonderful afternoon nap, we opened our home to a bunch of friends for dinner. Two of these dinner guests work at Starbucks and another one used to work at a different coffee shop. They were having a conversation about a few different and beautiful demitasses that customers had brought in from which to drink their espressos. I had no idea what a demitasse was. It turns out that it is a small cup like the type used for a double espresso or a Turkish coffee. Since I love both espresso and Turkish coffee, I have used a demitasse without knowing what it was called and always enjoyed it.

The hilarity of our dinnertime conversation came when it slowly dawned on me that they were talking about full-grown men who would take demitasses from their home and bring them to Starbucks to sit there and drink from cups from their own collection. They aren't talking about a large travel mug. This would make sense, especially for taking coffee in the car or for those concerned about the environment. In fact, they aren't talking about taking the drink to go at all. They were intentionally bringing little porcelain cups down to the coffee shop to drink it where they could be seen by everyone else.

As I began to ask questions about this, I began to get more and more agitated. For some reason, I was pissed that there were men out there who felt the need to do this. It wasn't bad that they were drinking out of a demitasse; as I said, I drink out of them and enjoy it thoroughly. My days of drinking boxed wine out of water glasses are a distant (and somewhat fuzzy) memory. These days, I appreciate having the proper glass for the drink. But it's not as if Starbucks doesn't have little cups there. Why in the hell would a man feel the need to do this? I couldn't understand, and I still can't!

I think this is simply the sad state of affairs when it comes to men. The spirit of masculinity has been crushed or worn away over time.

It's time for us to move away from this. It's time to check to see if you still have a pair. For the sake of our society, leave the damn demitasse at home and do something. Change the oil in your car, build a deck, climb a mountain, paint a picture, install new irrigation for the front yard, or get yourself to the gym. The world will always have new and better technology and experts. But what it really needs is the spirit of the man who is willing to go down swinging, who lives outside of his own head.

A man is more than a consumer, more than a collector!

MANHOOD AND THE TOTIN' CHIP

PAUL KOCH

Every now and then, I get a strong craving for hot wings. When I lived in Georgia, it was never much of an issue to satisfy such a longing, for there were incredible restaurants that were dedicated to the craft of making the perfect wings. And while you can certainly find good wings in California, you also find a lot of very average wings. While on a quick getaway with my wife, I spied a Buffalo Wild Wings and knew they offered great wings. In we went, and together we plowed through a pile of chicken wings smothered in various delicious sauces. As we were preparing to leave, I was approached by a large man dressed all in black. He looked like a security guard. In fact, that was exactly what he was.

He was polite and quietly referred to the metal clip fastened to my right pocked. He asked if it was a knife. I told him it was. (It was a Gerber multitool, but I don't think he would have cared about the distinction.) Then he said that I needed to leave it in my car. Now look, I wasn't trying to get on an airplane. I wasn't sneaking a knife into a ballgame around security screening. I was eating some wings with my wife. I'm sure there was a reason for such overzealous caution. Perhaps they'd had an incident before and were trying to prevent another problem—a sort of restaurant-level "Patriot Act." But the whole thing got me thinking about the values and fears of our society and about what happens when tools become viewed only as weapons.

For those of you who were in the Boy Scouts of America as children, you will no doubt remember the Totin' Chip card. This card was essentially your license to carry a pocketknife, swing an ax, or operate a saw. The rules were straightforward:

- Read and understand woods tools use and safety rules from the *Boy Scout Handbook*.
- Demonstrate proper handling, care, and use of the pocket knife, ax, and saw.
- Use knife, ax, and saw as tools, not playthings.
- Respect all safety rules to protect others.
- Respect property. Cut living and dead trees only with permission and good reason.
- Subscribe to the Outdoor Code.

After meeting the criteria, you were given a card, and no one worried about you carrying a pocketknife. This may sound like a small thing, but for me (and I assume many others), this was a rite of passage toward manhood. I joyfully tucked that card into my OP wallet with Velcro closure and began carrying a knife in my pocket at eleven years old. If any leader saw me failing to observe the safety rules for the knife, they would review the rules and then cut one of the corners off my Totin' Chip card. If all four corners were cut off, the privilege of carrying a knife, swinging an axe, or operating a saw was taken away.

As simple as it might seem, this whole process provided something crucial. To begin with, the knife, ax, or saw is viewed initially and intentionally as a tool. They are not weapons to be feared but crucial items to achieve essential goals in everyday life. In addition, the whole notion of the Totin' Chip taught young men not only that they *could* carry a pocketknife but that they *should* carry one. Carrying a tool was part of being a man, which means that there was a sense of self-reliance built into the whole endeavor. After all, why carry a tool if not to use it?

There is something inherently good about a certain amount of self-reliance. There is something invigorating about having some sort of mastery over the world. However, today we are constantly pressed into reliance on others, and not in a good way. We are not simply encouraged to seek out the gifts and wisdom of others to aid and guide our endeavors. Rather, we are told to outsource the whole job. Increasingly, everything from changing oil in a car, to installing a new light fixture, to chopping firewood is something that we are encouraged to leave to others, the experts who are properly qualified.

More and more, men today won't even give it a shot. They just assume that they should leave it to others. Everything around us reinforces the wisdom of such an approach. After all, when our phones don't work, we must take them in to the store. They can't fix it either. They simply sell you the new, upgraded version. When we open the hoods of our cars, we come face-to-face with another hood all together, one made of a mass of wires and emission standards–compliant components that we can never get through. This lack of spiritedness has infected the church as well. We hesitate to act far too often because we have been conditioned to wait for the approval of the experts.

I think it's time to reclaim our self-reliance. Even if we fail, let's go down swinging. Let's impart to our children a desire to have mastery over the things in their lives. Let's put our Totin' Chip cards back in our wallets. And when we are asked by some random "expert" to leave our pocketknife in the car, just take out that card and show them that at least a few corners haven't been cut off.

STRAPPED!

ROSS ENGEL

For twenty years now, I've had the same pair of companions accompanying me to the gym. My wife can't stand them. They're old and smell like sweat and maple syrup, but they push me beyond the limits of what I can do on my own. Well, today my wife can rejoice because those companions are no more. They ripped during my morning session in the gym.

For twenty years, this pair of lifting straps has accompanied me to the gym. When my grip would fail doing heavy deadlifts, weighted pullups, or some other heavy pulling exercise, I would put them on and keep adding more weight. The straps allowed me to keep lifting heavy stuff in the gym long after my hands couldn't grip the bar. They helped me push past my own limitations.

In pastoral ministry and in every arena of life, there are times when we are not able to do everything that we must do on our own. We do all we can do, push as far as we can push, and do as many of the tasks as humanly possible, and we still find ourselves coming up short. Limited by the amount of time we have, our own abilities, or even our own strength and fortitude, there comes a time when we just can't go it alone. It is in those times when we can't push ourselves any further that we need to have people on whom we can rely. We need people who can give us strength to keep going, help us step back from the edge so we can catch our breath, and help us overcome and work through our weaknesses.

I'm reminded of the account of Moses and the Israelites fighting against the Amalekites. Exodus 17:9–12 records this event in God's people's history. We are told that as long as Moses kept his hands raised high, the Israelites would prevail in battle. As soon as Moses let his weary arms drop, the Israelites would be overcome. To ensure victory, Moses needed help. He couldn't hold his hands aloft for the entire battle on his own, so Aaron and Hur stepped in. They put a stone under Moses for him to sit upon, and then the two men held his hands high. His hands were held steady by the help of these two men until the sun set and the battle was complete. Israel was victorious.

Aaron and Hur did the job that was given to Moses. They didn't tell Moses to take a spot on the bench while they took care of business. And Moses wasn't wimping out, looking to pass off his duties to someone else. He didn't delegate a task that he didn't want to do himself. But Moses was spent; he had reached his limits. He was exhausted, and yet the job wasn't finished. Aaron and Hur came to support Moses so that he could do his job. They didn't come to take Moses's place or subvert his authority. After all, it wasn't promised to them that their hands would create victory. They simply came to Moses's aid in his time of need and helped him complete the task given to him.

There is something here for both pastors and laypeople to consider. Brother pastors, it's hard to be in ministry alone. We are limited by the number of hours in a day and even our skill sets at times, and each week it seems that there is a smorgasbord of additional tasks that show up unannounced on our schedules. Most of us don't like to ask for help or even admit that we need it. Like strong-willed toddlers, we often like to imagine that we can do just fine on our own. We may be able to fake it for a while, but it isn't long before stress rises, frustrations start to boil over, and we run ourselves ragged. After all, we all have our limitations.

It's OK to ask for support from others, whether it's from brother pastors or compassionate laypeople.

Do hear me, brothers, and understand that I'm not encouraging you to shove off the tasks that you're supposed to be doing. I'm not telling you to deep-six the boring or unnoticed tasks that you're called to do, such as visiting the sick, teaching the young and old, and the dozen or so other things promised on the ordination vows listed on our Diplomas of Vocation. I am encouraging you to ask for help so that you can, as the holder of the Office of the Holy Ministry, accomplish the tasks that God has given you to do.

Beloved laypeople, please understand that your pastor probably won't readily admit that he needs help or that he's overwhelmed at times. At times, it might serve your pastor best if you just pop in and be a friend or ask if there is anything with which he needs some support. It is highly unlikely that your pastor will even admit that he has any limitations. After all, many pastors were educated in seminaries at a time when they were taught that pastors were expected to work eighty hours a week and had to prove each day to their congregations just how motivated and dedicated they were to their calling and ministerial tasks. I recall one professor even encouraged future pastors not to take their full vacation time for personal or family use. Rather, we were to use vacation time to plan the next six months of sermons and studies for the congregation.

A lot has changed since then. A word of caution: the pendulum has swung away from that model of "work yourself to death" ministry. But let us make sure that the pendulum doesn't swing so far that pastors end up thinking that they need someone to hold their hand throughout their ministry just so that they can do the very things they were trained to do.

It can be a tremendous comfort in this often isolated task of ministry to know that you have companions, folks who truly care about you and the ministry, who are willing to help strengthen you for your tasks. Just knowing that can be all the encouragement needed to keep pushing through the limits and accomplishing the tasks that have been prepared in advance for us to do.

Strap up, fellas. We've got some heavy lifting to do!

LESSONS FROM A SON

PAUL KOCH

This year, I traveled to Fort Wayne, Indiana, for the Thirty-Second Annual Symposium on Exegetical Theology and the Fortieth Annual Symposium on the Lutheran Confessions. These two conferences, hosted back-to-back at the seminary, are always packed full of great insights and discussions by top-notch scholars. To be sure, leaving the beautiful confines of Ventura, California to travel to Fort Wayne in the middle of January isn't always a joyful undertaking. Nonetheless, I go every year. I go for the opportunity to learn and so that I might be a better pastor and teacher; but most of all, I go because every year I gather together with a handful of very good friends. It's their presence, laughter, and banter in the bars late into the night that make it all worthwhile.

This year was especially fun. In addition to our usual schedule of things to do, we packed into a corner of the bar at Don Hall's Guesthouse and did a remote recording of *Ringside with the Preacher Men*. That night, *The Jagged Word* hosted all the fourth year seminarians as the band played late into the evening, and we toasted to their final months of study. We had a great time and created new stories that will be told for years to come, all while being bound together in a common confession and a clear understanding of who we are and why we gravitate toward one another.

When I find myself in the presence of true friends, there is an unnamed fire that is allowed to burn bright. It is found in our interactions—our laughs, jokes, and insults. It might be offensive to some or unpredictable to others, but it is part of the spirit of manhood and something most men long for.

The Friday that we headed home happened to be President Trump's inauguration. From newsfeeds on my phone to the monitors in the airport, I could see the spectacle unfold along with the protests against it all. I don't mind outspoken opposition, but I shake my head when I see grown men whine and complain about outcomes they don't support in a manner more suitable to preschool than a protest. I saw one clip of a guy screaming at the top of his lungs while falling to his knees as Trump was sworn in. Part of me thought, "How sad. I hope he has someone to care for him for he really seems to be hurting." And the other part of me thought, "What a pansy, throwing a temper-tantrum like a little boy who can't have a cookie."

Either way, I suppose I just felt sorry for him, ashamed, and embarrassed.

Now, *The Jagged Word* has enjoyed some success, but with that success comes those who would love for us to stop what we are doing or censor it. More than likely, most would have us get on board with their specific view and promote the comfortable echo chamber to which they've grown accustomed. I don't pay much attention to dissenters unless they have the courage to speak to me like a man. So if someone tells me about a Facebook post saying something about the character of the people who write for this blog, I simply imagine them as that snowflake screaming at the inauguration and I feel the same way about them.

On the flight home, I thought a lot about the state of masculinity in all this. From scholars presenting topics that may not be well received to young seminarians nervous about where they will be placed to take up the task of being the hitmen and midwives of God, from obscure bloggers trying to be part of a beneficial conversation to the mainstream media finding themselves on the outside looking in, from the rise of the podcast to the ubiquity of social media—what has this done to men? Real men, those who fight for honor, rally to their brother's cause, and are courageous and strong. Is there room for the strenuous life that shapes men in today's society? Do we value the face-to-face confrontation and the strength of the pack? Do we even care?

AND THEN I MADE IT HOME

PAUL KOCH

After being gone for a week, I entered my house to the loving embrace of my wife followed immediately by my four daughters hugging me back into the house. Then came the boy, my son (the youngest), who just turned seven. He gave me a sort of lame side hug then wanted to show me some pictures on which he had been working. But no sooner had I sat down on the couch than the assault began. He leaped onto my back from the arm of the couch, trying his best to get me into a chokehold. I threw him onto the floor, and for the next thirty minutes, it was on. Bodies flying were interspersed by charley horses and rear naked chokes. When he got tired of being my jiu-jitsu dummy, he opted for the Nerf guns. The battle moved around the living room and into the dining room.

Through the exhaustion and occasional shot of pain, the laughter never ceased. And when I finally smothered him until he tapped out, I was reminded of the great strength and hope of masculinity. This masculinity is not sorted out in cyberspace gossip circles but in the physical rising up of a son against the loving resistance of a father. You see, he reminds me that the fire that burns within is not some stray spark or some dying relic. Rather, it is the fuel that secures the bonds that matter in our lives.

The scholar, seminarian, social justice warrior, nameless blogger, and Facebook guardian of the truth can all learn something from a son. Rather, we can be reminded of the joy of the confrontation and the excitement of joining in the fight until we can no longer move—something we have forgotten. Instead of concealing the fire within, we can let it burn with those who we call friends and brothers.

SPIRITUAL MASTURBATION AND MASCULINITY

PAUL KOCH

In my experience, women fight differently than men. As a father of five, one boy and four girls, I have witnessed the clear difference in their strategies and tactics. My son seems to have a deep, instinctual desire to fight with a physical exchange, a trading of blows to make his point. In fact, you can see the torment he goes through when he restrains from physical retaliation toward one of his sisters because he has been taught not to hit girls from the get-go.

My daughters, on the other hand, engage in what I call "psychological warfare." They play with each other's emotions and learn how to push the right buttons through subtle manipulation to get the desired response. Without a single blow thrown, they can reduce a sibling to a mess of tears. For some reason, these wounds seem to last far longer and be more devastating than a simple punch to the nose, Indian burn, or pink belly.

The thing is, as our technologies and modern conveniences continue to advance, we find that a man's natural will to fight, his desire to prove his strength or courage or mastery over physical obstacles, is not only restrained today but even outmoded and unnecessary. Those traits of masculinity are then repressed and perverted. They don't go away. Rather, they are channeled to fake or virtual outlets. As I see it, we run the danger of becoming like Don Quixote, spending our days tilting at windmills while thinking we are actually attacking dragons. We play at war in video games and think we demonstrate honor and courage among our "friends" by a clever rebuttal on Facebook. And when it's time to exercise our sexual prowess, all we need is a high-speed Internet connection and a few moments alone.

In our civilized age, manhood is increasingly understood as some sort of masturbatory existence. More and more, men are disconnected from the physical. We spend more time inside our heads, and technology makes it easier and easier to stay there.

Take my vocation as an example. I think the study of theology in and of itself has a high propensity for encouraging our masturbatory existences. Men who engage in theological study can do so in a virtual world of their own creation—or at least a virtual world of their own choosing. They can be part of very specific groups of like-minded individuals, write blogs, and make clever remarks on Facebook without ever leaving their parents' basement. Theologians are civilized, so they don't have to fight like men. There is no real strength, courage, mastery, or honor needed. Instead, they engage in spiritual masturbation, in which they make themselves feel good by being right—at least within their own heads.

Spiritual masturbation is not about engaging with others or considering new metaphors, ideas, or cultural nuances. It's not expanding our bookshelves or challenging our preconceived notions. It's about feeling good, justifying ourselves, and being right.

Of course, we don't want to be wrong in our theology. We want to be faithful to the word. We desire to confess the true faith. But this is not the end of theology. The goal is not to be correct. Striving only to be correct leaves us in our own heads, ready to police the heretics in a virtual world so we can sleep better knowing the dragons are slain.

Rather, the goal of theology is the exercising of the word. It is the proclamation of the truth for the benefit of another. This ought to drive us out of our studies, away from our virtual communities, and into the lives of our neighbors. A masculine theologian ought not be afraid of the other but should welcome the engagement as an opportunity to exercise their skill and mastery. This is not a work of self-love, of spiritual masturbation, but of genuine love for the body of Christ.

> And he gave the apostles, the prophets, the evangelists, the shepherds and teachers, to equip the saints for the work of ministry, for building up the body of Christ, until we all attain to the unity of the faith and of the knowledge of the Son of God, to mature manhood, to the measure of the stature of the fullness of Christ, so that we may no longer be children, tossed to and fro by the waves and carried about by every wind of doctrine, by human cunning, by craftiness in deceitful schemes. Rather, speaking the truth in love, we are to grow up in every way into him who is the head, into Christ, from whom the whole body, joined and held together by every joint with which it is equipped, when each part is working properly, makes the body grow so that it builds itself up in love. (Eph. 4:11–16)

Every Sunday morning, as I go through my private ritual of putting on my vestments and preparing to lead worship, I pray Luther's famous Sacristy Prayer out loud. The third line says, "If Thou art pleased to accomplish anything through me, to Thy glory and not to mine or to the praise of men, grant me, out of Thy pure grace and mercy a right understanding of Thy Word and that I may also diligently perform it." The performance of the word is the goal. The application of law and gospel, the killing and resurrection of God, this is where our strength, courage, and mastery will come into play. The actual practice of these outside of my own head for the sake of my neighbor is where I find honor in my vocation.

In the end, I think we still need men who are willing to fight like men outside of their own heads and inside the messy lives of others.

"And how are they to believe in him of whom they have never heard? And how are they to hear without someone preaching?"

WALL BUILDING AS A CHRISTIAN VIRTUE

PAUL KOCH

Since the election of Donald Trump, there has been a national discussion about the legitimacy, legality, and virtue of building walls. Our politicians, comedians, talk show hosts, and Super Bowl ads have taken up this discussion: Is the idea of building a wall driven by fear, racism, patriotism, or some combination of all the above? Is it something that is inherent to the idea of what it means to be an American? Is it a shameful move toward Nazi-era hate speech? Will a wall make America great again, or will it redefine her as something of which we can no longer be proud?

It's interesting to watch this discussion unfold among the pundits, journalists, and barflies. In the end, I think it will speak loudly about what America is and how it will be perceived among the nations of the world. But it has also caused me to think about the building of walls around much smaller, more tight-knit groups within the United States. While I'm not sure what it will mean for a nation the size and scope of the United States to build a wall, I do think there is a place for walls within the empire.

There is something good, something virtuous, about building a wall around a family, tribe, or church.

I finally read Cormac McCarthy's monumental tale *The Road*. It has haunted my mind since I finished it. He tells the story of a man and his son in burned-out America carefully making their way to the coast to flee the dead of winter. Along the way, he paints a picture of the fears and strengths of manhood and fatherhood and what it means to continue to carry the fire. Throughout the story, there is a scene that plays out, a set of actions that occurs again and again. Every time this unnamed father and son stop to make camp for the night, the father sets out and walks the perimeter. He trudges through the snow and ash to make sure that where they've settled is safe. On the inside of that perimeter is his life; inside is food, water, shelter, and most importantly, his child. Outside is death, destruction, and those who would take what he is charged to protect. Again and again, he walks the perimeter. In the middle of the night, when some sound stirs him from sleep, he walks the perimeter. In the morning, as they warm some coffee over a small fire, he will again walk the perimeter. The reader learns quite clearly that there is an inside and an outside, an "us" versus "them."

If he could have built a wall, he would have. All that mattered to him was who was on the inside of the perimeter.

I'm not saying that this will work for a nation with the breadth of the United States, but I do think it is worthy of our consideration in regards to the church. Today, it is common to speak lovingly of churches as having no walls, as being inclusive and welcoming to any and all. Membership, if it happens at all, is a mere formality, and people tend to treat the church as a voluntary organization that they can choose to be a part of or leave at any minor inconvenience. There tends to be little separation between those on the inside and those on the outside, between "us" and "them." In fact, I would venture to guess that most Christians wouldn't even like the language (at least publicly) of us versus them.

If people make a distinction between those inside the perimeter and those outside of it, it is usually based on morality and not confession of faith. The "us" becomes those who act like Christians, doing Christian things in Christian ways. The "them" are all the sinners out there shunning the Christian ways and openly sinning.

But it hasn't always been this way.

The baptismal liturgy that we use in my church includes a beautiful prayer commonly called the "Flood Prayer," which was originally composed by Martin Luther. It is a petition to God on behalf of the one about to be washed in the waters of baptism. The last section goes like this: "Grant that they be kept safe and secure in the holy ark of the Christian Church, being separated from the multitude of unbelievers and serving your name at all times with a fervent spirit and a joyful hope, so that, with all believers in Your promise, they would be declared worthy of eternal life."

This image of baptism is one of separation, of being brought to the inside, becoming one of "us" as distinct from one of "them." The "us" is established by the work of our Lord through the faithful proclamation and administration of the sacraments. The "us" is important because it not only defines who is on our side but also gives strength and courage to any work done outside the perimeter.

I think there is something good about building this type of wall and clarifying exactly who we are. It gives clarity of purpose for any engagement outside the wall, even while protecting those vulnerable within.

ON RECEIVING CRITICISM

HOW WELL DOES THE CRITIC TAKE HIS OWN MEDICINE?

SCOTT KEITH

The ritual of an Inklings was unvarying. When half a dozen or so had arrived, tea would be produced, and then when pipes were well alight Jack would say, "well has nobody got anything to read us?" Out would come a manuscript, and we would settle down to sit in judgment upon it—real unbiased judgment, too, since we were no mutual admiration society: praise for good work was unstinted, but censure for bad work—or even not so good work—was often brutally frank. To read to the Inklings was a formidable ordeal.

—WARNIE LEWIS (OLDER BROTHER OF C. S. LEWIS)

A good friend of mine has a manuscript that she wishes to publish someday. This friend is a solid thinker and a good writer, and I am sure her work will add a great deal to the body of work already existent on her topic. But she is unsure of what to do with her book. She asked me, "What do I do with my little work?"

"First, you have to let us read it," I said.

Sharing something dear to you, something that you have poured your heart and soul into, is not easy. Yet the worst thing that can happen to a work of such care is that it be hidden, kept away, refused the praise and the criticism of its readers. The idea that someone might take your hard work and dismiss it as inconsequential or even bad is one of the most terrifying thoughts that any writer faces. But lack of exposure will not make a bad text good, just as exposure to criticism will not make a good text bad.

Getting over the fear of criticism is more easily said than done. My book *Being Dad: Father as a Picture of God's Grace* was recently reviewed on a well-known fatherhood website, fathervision.com. The review is thorough, honest, scathingly unbiased in its assessment, and often accurate in its criticism. At the end of the day, the author of the review recommends my book with comments like this: "But those who come to this book looking for inspiration in the noble calling of fatherhood and for encouragement to keep pressing into the sacred work of fathering will come away from this book with some very good food for thought."

Rest assured, this praise did not stop the author from cleaning my clock on other areas of the work. Among other things, he criticizes my distinctly Lutheran approach to the topic, saying that: "As a non-Lutheran reader, I felt like I was 'out of the club' so to speak. This also included the constant and annoying bifurcation between 'Law and Grace.' The author is too immersed in his own thought bubble." In some ways, I think he is right. Even if he is not, I need to hear him and think that he might be. Though, I might also encourage the reviewer to remember that we all have a "thought bubble" and to use my book as an opportunity to get out of his own for a few hours.

Though now highly regarded as a great Christian author and teacher, in his time, C. S. Lewis was often criticized for what he wrote. He received the criticism that his works seemed hastily constructed or that they only flirted with being scholarly. Even his friends said that Lewis would introduce difficult theological concepts only to conclude them in too short a work, allowing the tensions inherent to these difficult topics to stand unresolved. The reader can get a sense of how Lewis reacted to some of these critics as he responds to the criticism of *The Pilgrim's Regress* in the appendix to the third edition of that work. Lewis is a total gentleman as he glides through the objections to his work point by point, praising the accurate criticism and taking the blame for where the work fell short.

As a budding author, I need the type of criticism Warnie Lewis describes above: "real unbiased judgment." We have too many people in our lives that serve as our mutual admiration society. Withholding accurate criticism will not make those around us more self-aware or improve their self-esteem. Rather, we will create a world full of people who believe that they are better than they are.

Imagine a world full of writers who cannot write, teachers who do not know their field, musicians unworthy of the title, and artists who produce trash praised as life-changing epitaphs that will stand in perpetuity as hallmarks of culture and intellectual sophistication. Perhaps you do not need to imagine it. Perhaps all that is needed is for us to look around at our mediocre world and cast an examining gaze at it through clear eyes to see the lies.

Worse yet, how will we Christians tell a world full of people who are wholly unaccustomed to criticism on even the most mundane of topics that they are sinful in thought, word, and deed? Bringing people to Christ involves two messages: God's law ("For all have sinned and fall short of the glory of God" [Rom. 3:23]) and God's gospel ("and are justified by his grace as a gift, through the redemption that is in Christ Jesus" [Rom. 3:24]).

To go through life without allowing those we love, those who are close to us, or those that know our field well to analyze us and our work critically is akin to walking through this early life blind and unaided. The message of the law is a shock to the system for all of us, more so if we have never been corrected or criticized. The message of the gospel is foolishness, and it's even more foolish if it's equated to the chorus of false praise that the world seems to send our way in a daily fashion.

To my friend, show us your work. Praise for good work will be unstinted, but censure for bad work—or even not-so-good work—will probably be brutally frank. And that is the way it should be.

Finally, I give a heartfelt thank you to the reviewer at fathervision.com for reviewing *Being Dad*. The work you do at fathervision.com is important and valuable. God's richest blessing to you as you continue serving Him who has called you out of the darkness into His marvelous light.

GROWING OLD

SCOTT KEITH

> Those who lack within themselves the means for living a blessed and happy life will find any age painful. But for those who seek good things within themselves, nothing imposed on them by nature will seem troublesome. Growing older is a prime example of this. Everyone hopes to reach old age, but when it comes, most of us complain about it. People can be so foolish and inconsistent.
>
> —CICERO, *HOW TO GROW OLD*

've been thinking about growing old lately. Maybe it's because I just became a grandpa. Nonetheless, all my contemplation has reminded me that we are culturally obsessed with staying young. We work out to avoid growing old. We follow every fad thrown at us by pseudoscience to stave off any wrinkle, gray hair, or slight physical impediment. We seem to define our youth with vim, vigor, and vitality, and old age with fatigue, apathy, and weakness.

During a trip to New York City, I visited the world-renowned Strand Books. If you haven't visited Strand Books, you ought to, as it is a truly remarkable experience. Their slogan is "18 Miles of Books." Strand Books is just my kind of place. When I am in a bookstore like Strand Books, I am always on the lookout for something I don't have and something "unique," as defined by something that I would not intentionally search for on Amazon.

While there, I ran across and purchased a little work by Marcus Tullius Cicero entitled *How to Grow Old*. (The side benefit for me is that this copy, translated by Philip Freeman, is an English/Latin edition that allows me to safely practice my Latin.) This is a great little work, produced by Rome's arguably most famous orator and senator. He composed this book after he had opposed Julius Caesar's marching into Rome with his troops. Caesar had pardoned Cicero for his seeming betrayal, but Cicero was humiliated and retired to his home in the country. By this time, Cicero had been divorced twice, was getting older, and was out of a job. All accounts suggest that he was feeling somewhat forlorn and even useless.

It is during this time that Cicero found purpose in writing. While he was retired at his country home, he penned some of his greatest works. *How to Grow Old* is not usually considered among Cicero's greatest works, though it was the first of his works to be translated into English and published in America.

In his little work, Cicero lays out ten lessons—you have to love ancient ten-step programs—that we all need to learn in life in preparation of growing old:

1. A good old age begins in youth.
2. Old age can be a wonderful part of life.
3. There are proper seasons to life.
4. Older people have much to teach the young.
5. Old age need not deny an active life, but we need to accept limitations.
6. The mind is a muscle that must be exercised.
7. Older people must stand up for themselves.
8. Sex is highly overrated. (I'm not sure I agree with this one.)
9. Cultivate your own garden. (Have a hobby or take care of something that you care about.)
10. Death is not to be feared.

So what are we to make of Cicero's ten-step program? Well, I hear in it not only ancient wisdom toward living a virtuous life but also echoes of what the scriptures teach all of us.

1. "Train up a child in the way he should go; even when he is old he will not depart from it" (Prov. 22:6).
2. "He took his last breath and died at a ripe old age, old and contented, and he was gathered to his people" (Gen. 25:8).
3. "For everything there is a season, and a time for every matter under heaven" (Eccles. 3:1).
4. "Hear this, you elders; listen, all you inhabitants of the land. Has anything like this ever happened in your days or in the days of your ancestors? Tell your children about it, and let your children tell their children, and their children the next generation" (Joel 1:2–3).
5. "He gives power to the faint, and to him who has no might he increases strength" (Isa. 40:29).
6. "Be sober-minded; be watchful. Your adversary the devil prowls around like a roaring lion, seeking someone to devour" (1 Pet. 5:8).
7. "Do not rebuke an older man, but exhort him as a father, younger men as brothers, older women as mothers, and with all propriety" (1 Tim. 5:1–2).
8. "Flee from sexual immorality. Every other sin a person commits is outside the body, but the sexually immoral person sins against his own body" (1 Cor. 6:8).
9. "They shall still bring forth fruit in old age" (Ps. 92:14).
10. "For I am persuaded that neither death nor life, nor angels nor rulers, nor things present, nor things to come, nor powers, nor height, nor depth, nor any other created thing will have the power to separate us from the love of God that is in Christ Jesus our Lord!" (Rom. 8:38–39).

At the end of the day, this little work convinced me that even wise pagans like Cicero knew something that we all—Christians too—neglect. Getting older is the way of things and is not to be feared. After all, we have nothing left to fear; Christ has taken all our real fears upon Himself. He has conquered sin, death, and the devil; now, the lives we live are lived in Christ. When our old age results in our deaths, and it will, death will not have the last word. Christ has ripped death's last word out of its mouth and has declared that you will live again because of His death and resurrection. The lives we now live—even the lives we live as we get older—are lived in the freedom of that truth. Christ is risen, and because He is risen, we shall be risen indeed! Thus the words of Cicero quoted in the beginning can be adjusted to have new meaning for those in Christ: "But for those who seek good things in *Christ*, nothing imposed on them by nature will seem troublesome. Growing older is a prime example of this."

WANT TO BE AN AMERICAN SNIPER?

JOEL HESS

When I saw the movie *American Sniper* with some of my high school students, I was moved more deeply and permanently than I have been in some time. As many of you know, it's about Chris Kyle, the record-holding Navy SEAL sniper who, ironically if not poetically, was killed by someone he was trying to help. Clint Eastwood, one of my favorite actors and directors, flawlessly portrayed Kyle's tours in Iraq and his difficulties assimilating into civilian life. It was not an artistic film. It was not Eastwood's cleverest endeavor. No, Eastwood disappeared and simply let the story tell itself, which may be a greater accomplishment than directing with heavy, Van Gogh–like strokes.

When the film ended, no one in the audience said a word. As the credits rolled, they left silently, like at the end of a Good Friday service. Everyone was blown away. And I am sure that I am not the only one who asked existential questions: Who am I? What am I doing with my life? In between tours, as he rode with his wife to go shopping, Kyle lamented, "There's a war out there, and I'm driving to the mall." This strange juxtaposition Americans enjoy hit me square in the face. How can you laugh when people are dying? How can you waste time playing video games about the war while people are risking their lives in real war? How can you relax while others are suffering?

Fortunately, before I began to drive to the nearest navy recruiting center, I enjoyed an epiphany. This movie was not really about the war on terror. It did not glorify war, nor was its purpose to simply demonize terrorists. The film wasn't even about being a soldier or a sniper. Finally, it wasn't a rah-rah "thank God I'm an American and you suck" movie. This movie is about a man doing something that he saw needed to be done. He saw an opportunity to serve his fellow man and signed up, not for glory, a vision of grandeur, or to leave a legacy, but simply because it was the right thing to do. "God, country, family," he told a fellow soldier who was doubting why he was there. For Chris Kyle, there was no choice; his neighbor needed him. How fitting that he died not on the battlefield but at home helping out a mentally disturbed fellow soldier. Evil is everywhere. Sin is everywhere. Suffering is everywhere. People need help everywhere! You have neighbors going through their own wars on terror as they fight cancer, suffer abuse, or battle their own sinful desires. What are you going to do about it?

What I admire about Chris Kyle is not his marksmanship or various other skills. Rather, I admire how he loved his neighbors, his brothers-in-arms, and his wife and kids. On this day, as we remember the work of Martin Luther King Jr., the same can be admired of him.

This is the mark of heroism and valor that can be exercised by everyone in every vocation. You don't have to be a Navy SEAL to be a hero. You don't have to go overseas and fall on an IED to save your brothers to be a hero. You don't have to tell everyone your dream on the steps of the Lincoln Memorial. Whatever you have been given to do, as I told one youth, "Chris Kyle it!" Do it to the best of your ability and do it to the end.

Of course, this points to a hero who single-handedly served and saved both King and Kyle, Christ our Lord. He loved not only His neighbors but even His enemies: you and me, sinners, blasphemers, part-time heroes and part-time cowards. He loved us to the end, not for fame or glory, not to be praised or remembered, but to lift us up out of this war-torn, lonely existence and into His promised land. This peace and salvation empower us to stick our necks out, to take a risk in loving and serving others. No matter what happens, we shall rise on the last day when Christ comes again. And this isn't just a dream; it is the reality that is already in motion. Come, Lord Jesus.

WHERE IS ALL
∧ THE COOL STUFF?

PART TWO
WORKING FOR
OUR NEIGHBORS

WHY AREN'T ∧
YOU IN SCHOOL?

PASSION IS ∧
OVERRATED

WE DON'T
∧NEED SPORTS

∧ THE GARAGE
VS.
THE MAN CAVE

RADIATORS
∧ AND HAIR BUNS

∧ OLD BOOKS AND
NEW PULPITS

THE GRANITE ∧
NEVER LIES

WHERE IS ALL THE COOL STUFF?

SCOTT KEITH

Awhile back, I took a trip with my son Caleb and his best friend Quincy to Arizona. In between helping my mother-in-law clean out her old house, we took it upon ourselves to peruse some of the ubiquitous antique stores that are so prevalent in the greater Mesa area. These stores seem to overflow with items from the past that were made with care, a sense of craftsmanship, and quality. Thus these "antiques" still exist, are purchasable, and remain unique and attractive. In days gone by, even something as simple as .22 long rifle ammunition from the Winchester Company was purchased in a wooden box of such quality that the box could be resold today for five dollars.

By way of clarification, I would like to say that I am generally a fan of a modified minimalist lifestyle. By saying that I am a "minimalist," I mean that I am a fan of thrift and quality over quantity. To be sure, I like my stuff. I like clothes, books, outdoor gear, pipes, and all the general household accoutrements that make up a comfortable life and home. But again, I am a fan of quality. I believe that owning quality belongings is one of the odd pleasures that make an earthly existence more enjoyable than not. I don't necessarily like having more than I "need" of any of these things. Here lies the moral dilemma.

We have an overabundance of stuff in our lives. Our overcommercialized Walmart culture has made everything we own fast, cheap, and easy. We have more stuff than we will ever use, and it is expendable and disposable. We are inundated with a distinct lack of craftsmanship and have traded in the idea of owning a few nice things for owning many items that are more easily tossed into the rubbish bin than kept. In short, it is not the fact that we have more than we need, or even want more than we need, that is so troublesome. Rather, it is the reality that these desires seem to arise in us because we know that what we own is more crap than quality that causes us to desire more and more.

Therefore, in addition to being drawn to antique stores selling quality items of the past, I'm also drawn to the modern artisan movement. Modern artisanal craftsmen are people who have realized that we live in a disposable world and are attempting to do something about it. These are individuals who produce quality. There are now many denim manufacturers who have learned to make denim jeans as they were made in the 1950s by machines that were built in the 1930s or 1940s. Others are craftsmen like Dave at Saddleback Leather Co., who taught himself to craft and tool leather and who produces leather bags that will last a lifetime. As he says, "These are the bags your grandchildren will fight over when you are dead." Also, there are pipe makers like Smio Satou of Japan who have learned to craft pipes in the Dunhill style, by hand, producing more than an instrument for smoking tobacco; to them, a pipe is also a work of art and a pleasure that will last a lifetime. These are craftsmen who have refused to be, as Chesterton describes, "the wage slaves of modern industrialism" (Chesterton, *What's Wrong with the World*).

The difficulty is that these items are expensive. Perhaps you would argue that designating myself as thrifty is contradictory to buying things that are expensive. On the contrary, I believe that quality is worth the expense when possible and that purchasing one expensive item that will last a lifetime is thriftier than buying twenty that only last three years or fewer. Furthermore, I believe that supporting craftsmen in their trade is worth the extra expense. Vocation is not just a matter of completing a task in expectation of remuneration. Vocation involves serving others through action in a qualitative way. Further, I have no compunction whatsoever in saying that if I ever have the pleasure of buying a new Smio Satou pipe or finding an estate Dunhill in an antique store, they will serve me in a qualitative way until the day I die. So, where is all the cool stuff of yesteryear? Try an antique store; better yet, support a modern artisanal craftsman. Therein you will encounter the work of those who have produced quality in their vocation and those rare few who are yet attempting to do the same.

WHY AREN'T YOU IN SCHOOL?

VOCATION AND THE WORK OF THE HANDS

JOSH KEITH

Hello, I'm Josh Keith. Yes, it's another Keith. It's hard to throw a rock around these parts and not hit a Keith. My father, Scott, asked me if I would write something for *The Jagged Word*, so I decided to write about a question I'm commonly asked. This question comes up nearly daily, whether it's from people at the ACE Hardware where I work or the church I attend. It's always the same question: "Oh, you're eighteen? Aren't you in college?" By now I'm now accustomed to answering, "No, I had a couple of jobs during high school, learned to work with my hands, and liked it. After I graduated, I moved out of my parents' home and got a new job, and I'm doing my best to earn a living." What bothers me most is the judgment that comes after I respond. The faces of shock, pity, and disbelief get old quickly.

For those wondering why I've chosen not to go to school, for starters, let me just say that I have nothing against those who choose to further their formal education. For many, even for most, college seems like the best opportunity to broaden their academic education and apply what they learn to their future vocations. What I believe is wrong is the assumption—the expectation—that everyone my age should be in college and that there must be something wrong with those who aren't.

I don't think there's anything wrong with people who don't go to college. Even though I have not gone to college, I am trying to do the same thing as those who have—apply what I've learned to my vocation. As mentioned, I had a couple of jobs during high school. I worked at a glass shop installing windows and doors. I worked at a cabinet shop building and installing counters and cabinets. I spent time interning in a bike shop learning to assemble and repair bicycles. I didn't pick up these jobs just because I needed the money, though it was a nice bonus.

There were never dull days working in those shops, lifting hundreds of pounds of wood, glass, and metal. The most exciting day of work I had was when I was halfway up a two-story metal ladder during a thunderstorm. The more experienced partner was safely inside, holding the window I was installing in place. I was totally invigorated. Regardless of any shitty days, I kept those jobs because they seemed to teach me more than my "real" classes.

I learned that I love working with my hands and that I love the feeling of coming home sweaty and dusty from a hard day of work. I enjoy walking through the door, laying on the floor, and feeling the ache in my back that runs like ice water down my spine. I understand that these things do not sound appealing to everyone, especially in our day and age. However, I can say that it's a real shame that it's not appealing to more. I wish that I knew more people who feel the same as I do. I believe that the results of hard work, even when not printed as a letter grade on a test or paper, are worthy of praise. Learning to build things, working with hands, and serving people are noble endeavors and laudable vocational pursuits. I love the work I do. I love any opportunity

I get to help people with the knowledge and skills I've acquired. In the end, whether by means of college or not, isn't that what everyone wants? I want to show pride in my vocation of serving God by serving my neighbors through the movements of my everyday life at home and at work.

PASSION IS OVERRATED

JOSH KEITH

Okay, hear me out before you scoff and turn the page. I have many passions. From the adrenaline rush of setting up anchor and climbing a mountain face to the overly nerdy conversations of new Marvel movies to come, I would never give up my passions. Here's the kicker: don't follow your passions. Now, what I mean by this is that too many people nowadays don't understand what passion is or what it should be. Passion is happiness. It's finding something to love, but we have a bit of a crisis going on these days. People my age don't know how to work toward anything but their passions.

One of my childhood and adulthood heroes is Mike Rowe. If you haven't heard of him, you should look up the TV show *Dirty Jobs*. This show starred Mike Rowe and the people of America who do the toughest and dirtiest jobs in America—sewer cleaning, pest control, construction, fireworks making, and, my personal favorite, ostrich farming. He did all the jobs that most people these days wouldn't even want to consider as a career, and that's the problem. Ever since I started working at sixteen, I have constantly been asked if I am going to go to college. Anyone who asks this and hears my answer of "No, I'm actually working forty or more hours and following my career" is shocked and almost appalled. They ask with worry in their voices if I plan on going soon, then they try to convince me that I should go. I'm proud to say that I'm a rarity. At the same time, it's a shame to think that being a working individual at my age isn't up to par. And what astounds me more is that people my age are completely convinced that a degree in a certain field guarantees them their dream job.

Millions of young adults are met with what Mike Rowe calls "the dirty truth" (Rowe, "Don't Follow Your Passion"). Being passionate about something doesn't necessarily mean it should be your career. Rather, when you work hard and well enough at something, you become passionate about it. This truth never sets in for people my age. If it does, it's after tens of thousands of dollars in debt and a job at Starbucks that they are met with the reality that their dream job is most likely only that—a dream.

Jobs for the hardworking are out there, ripe for the taking. All they require is that you find pride in the completion of something that isn't easy—to be more than another fish in the sea of liberal arts majors and instead be the fisherman. So for all young adults out there who struggle in picking their expected major, there are always jobs out there for those who seek hard work, pride, and a vocation. And always remember that there's no shame in the old mentality of blood, sweat, and tears and that it's time for us "to get ready to get dirty," in the words of Mike Rowe.

WE DON'T NEED SPORTS

BOB HILLER

n a conversation with some old friends about why I like sports, they could only see the negative impact of sports on culture, higher education, and the church. They weren't fans. Though I vehemently tried to defend the benefits of sports, much of what they said resonated with me: What is wrong with sports? Or rather, what is wrong with our attitude toward them? Is there something wrong with playing and watching sports? Are sports nothing more than an idol that needs to be smashed? Maybe, but idolatry is too easy an answer. Idols are typically made out of the good parts of creation. So if sports are an idol, then there is something good about them that we are twisting and abusing. So why sports? Why do we need them? Do we need them at all? These questions brought me back to Chesterton and alcohol.

In his delightful book *Heretics*, G. K. Chesterton writes on the problem with a puritanical view of alcohol. Prohibition sought to rid us of alcoholism by removing all forms of booze. Drinking for pleasure would lead to all forms of "fornical kaboodelin'," as Dr. Rosenbladt used to say. However, some suggested alcohol could be used when *needed* for medical reasons. In response, Chesterton says:

> *The one genuinely dangerous and immoral way of drinking wine is to drink it as a medicine . . . Drink because you are happy, but never because you are miserable. Never drink when you are wretched without it, or you will be like the grey-faced gin-drinking in the slum; but drink when you would be happy without it you will be like the laughing peasant of Italy. Never drink because* **you need it,** *for this is rational drinking, and the way of death and hell. But drink because you do not need it, for this is irrational drinking, and the ancient health of the world.* (Chesterton, Heretics, *41–42)*

So the problem with drinking is not that people do it for fun but that they need it. Wine gladdens the heart of man, but it becomes dangerous once the heart needs wine to be glad.

Let's bring this sort of logic back to my question about the good of sports. Sports are games aimed at joy. For our existence, they are needless. Yet that is where their virtues lie. They bring recreation, pleasure, fun, and, of course, exercise, which is important for health. They can be useful in teaching healthy forms of competition and teamwork. When we "imbibe" sports for these reasons, they serve their purpose and are good for us. However, they are not *necessary* for any of these. We've made sports something they were never meant to be: necessary. When sports are a necessity, they enter "the way of death and hell."

Think about the way we treat Little League baseball. Some parents are convinced that their children need to be successful at Little League baseball in order to get into college. They start teaching eight-year-olds how to throw sliders and curve balls. By the time they are eighteen, they have some pretty filthy stuff (that's a compliment in baseball), which could mean a scholarship or the Minor League. They needed to learn to pitch that well that early on in order to have success at eighteen. However, placing such stress on children's arms can lead to Tommy John surgery by twenty-two. From that point on, their careers are shaky at best. For what it's worth, of all the eight-year-olds throwing split-finger breaking balls, a minuscule percentage have a prayer at going anywhere beyond high school.

But don't fret. Colleges still will look at team participation on college applications. By placing children in youth sports leagues, their chances of getting into schools increase. In other words, they need to play sports to secure their future. At this point, actual necessities are denied to children, such as quality time with family; disorganized, imaginative play; and of course, church attendance. I can break the third commandment far more easily if I know soccer helps my kid get into college. Who cares about fun or Bible stories? My eight-year-old has a future to consider!

On a much more terrifying level, consider a past case involving the University of Tennessee. Multiple women have come forth in a lawsuit against the school claiming that they were sexually assaulted by athletes. At the risk of hearsay, I will not get into the details of the case. However, I will speak to one thing that disturbs me to the core. After allegations were made against the school, sixteen coaches from various programs rallied together to stand up for the athletic department and school. They wanted to demonstrate there was a healthy culture on campus and support their administration. Women's soccer coach Brian Pensky said: "It was time for us to be strong. We came to the administration several weeks ago and said we want to put our faces out there and let people know that we're behind the decisions being made within this athletic department. Instead of us continuing to lie down and just kind of take it and take the beating, we felt like as a coaching unit we wanted our administration to know that we have their back and we have each other's back and our student-athletes' backs" (Low, "Tennessee Volunteers").

Are you not going to "lie down and take it," Mr. Pensky? This guy realizes that this is a sexual assault case, doesn't he? He realizes that young women were violently harmed, right? Good heavens.

Do you see the fear at the University of Tennessee? Instead of doing the right thing and saying, "We're suspending all athletics and pouring everything we have into getting these women the help and healing they need," the coaches trot out to defend the school for fear of losing athletics, something the school desperately *needs* for revenue. Their need for sports trumps justice and, more important, the well-being of these women. This is deeply disturbing.

I want my kids to enjoy sports. I want to play catch with my boys, have them hit whiffle balls at my face, and listen to them laugh hysterically. I want them to be angry at losing so that they try harder next time. I want there to be joy when we yell at the football game together. I want my kids to love sports, and that's why I fear putting them in a league. They don't need sports and neither do any of us. To lift from Chesterton, we *need* to return to the "irrational drinking" of play.

THE GARAGE VS. THE MAN CAVE

PAUL KOCH

A garage is a special thing, at least for me. For you, perhaps it's just a glorified parking spot or an overstuffed storage closet. But my garage is something more. I've never used a garage to store a vehicle as intended. Rather, it has always been a place of activity. It is a place of busted knuckles, colorful language, and loud music from my high school days blaring through a beat-up boom box covered in dust and oil residue.

After leaving my father's garage, my first garage was the one attached to our home in Georgia. It was a small, one-car garage in which things were placed with the careful imagination of a Tetris master. I had managed to build a small but adequate workbench. I had a vise, a wonderful drill press (I love that thing), welder, tool chest, and assorted power tools. I had to back my motorcycle out into the driveway to get any significant work done, but it was a place of comfort and escape.

Let me clarify. By escape, I don't mean that it was a place of hiding away. It was not a place where I could sneak off to have a beer or a smoke. It was not a spot established by the wife that I could decorate how I saw fit. My garage was not a so-called "man cave." I've grown to hate that term. From what I can gather, a man cave is a place where a man can act like he's at the bar without going to the bar, with a pool table (check), beer cooler (check), dart board (check), big screen TV, and place to congregate with other men (check and check). Just go to the damn bar! Bars are fun. But to escape to the garage is to engage in activity with purpose, to work by hand to produce something of quality that will stand outside of the mind.

I don't think we appreciate how powerful this production can be. Whether wrenching on a car, building a chair, or shimming up a new door, the content of the mind impacts the world. It can then be measured and tested. Its quality can be established. Such experiences are part of the fuel that gives a man his courage, vigor, and spirit.

Some of my fondest memories in that garage are from when I was tearing down and rebuilding my motorcycle. I stripped my '89 Harley down to the frame, rebuilt the motor, completely rewired it, chopped it up here and there to create the "look" I was going for, and even got pretty good at laying down my own pinstripes. After dinner, I would grab a beer and head for the garage. Some nights I would lose track of all time. Lost in a rhythm of welding, grinding, and rewelding (I'm not the best welder), I'm sure I kept up my neighbors with all the racket coming from my garage. Before she went to bed, my lovely wife would finally pop her head in to remind me of the time. After all, I did have to get up and go to work in the morning.

More and more, it seems that the world is comfortable with losing this experience. Whether mechanical work, woodwork, or just about every other sort of craftsmanship imaginable, we rely especially on the professionals to do the job. Everything has a "hood" that only a certain few can get through. It used to be that everyday people could open the hoods of their cars, sort things out, and make their way through the components, wires, and hoses. These days, after opening the hood, a whole other hood lies underneath—one of complicated wires, self-diagnostic systems, and computer-assisted driving modules. The signal is loud and clear: only professionals have business being under there. I'm typing this on a computer, but I hardly understand how it works. Others may be reading this on phones that they couldn't dream of recreating. The whole discussion of quality becomes the property of companies and factories, and the average man is left to sort through online reviews to make his choice.

Instead of garages, we have man caves where men gather to escape through inactivity. They tell stories of the good old days as they laugh at YouTube videos and share their latest experiences at the electronics superstore. We have forgotten what it feels like to fire up a rebuilt motor for the first time and that it's possible to do anything with enough work. And we've forgotten what it is to fail, not through disappointment and laziness, but when our thoughts wouldn't play out in the world—when our effort to do what we thought we could wasn't good enough and we are sent back to the drawing board to learn from our mistakes and try again.

For me, it has been far too long since I've been in the garage. This past weekend, we finally cleaned it out. I built my new workbench, bolted down my drill press (have I mentioned that I love that thing?), and began organizing all the tools. Last night, I walked out there just to smell it and stand for a moment, imagining all that could be done with such a great space. It's time to wake from the slumber of our man caves and get back to work!

RADIATORS AND HAIR BUNS

PAUL KOCH

When my 2000 Jeep Grand Cherokee began to over-heat, I pulled into a parking lot near home to look for the problem. I found a small river of coolant pouring from the water pump and pooling beneath the vehicle. I risked driving it the rest of the way home but knew that my Tuesday would be spent covered in grease and grime.

By Wednesday morning, my vehicle was on the road again after I replaced the entire cooling system—the radiator, water pump, and thermostat. I also changed the transmission fluid and filter.

After it was all done, I was asked by a friend if I liked doing that kind of work. I found the answer wasn't all that easy. I didn't like spending my day lying on my back covered in transmission fluid. I didn't like making three trips to the auto-parts store. I didn't like busting my knuckles when the torque wrench slipped off a housing bolt. But I love the quiet victory of being able to master my own stuff.

It wasn't just that I fixed the problem. Sure, that was the inten-tion, but it was more that I gave it a shot. I opened the garage door, pondered the Chilton's repair manual, took a deep breath, and began to turn the wrench on stubborn bolts. Even if I had failed to fix it and had to take it to an expert, I would have found some joy in knowing that I went down swinging. That is what I like, and I have found that I like it more and more.

But this doesn't just apply to turning wrenches. For a while, I had to take my youngest daughter to her ballet class. Not only did I need to make sure she was dressed and ready to go, but I also had to put her hair up. And I'll be damned if I wasn't going to figure out how to master the ballet bun. Trust me: at times it was easier to change out a water pump than to control all the flyaway hairs and get the bobby pins to stay. I even watched You-Tube videos for tips and tricks. By the end, I was pretty good at it.

I fear we have become accustomed to deferring to others, not just with our stuff, but with our various callings in life. Too often, we don't even try to master our own craft, whatever it may be. Instead, we settle for mediocrity with a few gems that we've stolen from Pinterest or our Twitter feed to spruce up our work. What happened to the pursuit of quality? What happened to the drive to be the best at what we do? What happened to the willingness to risk failure so that we might be better in the end?

It's time to take some risks. It's time to shake off the dull sloth of what this world gives us and dare to master the stuff within our control. If you're a mother, then be one that breaks the mold. If you're a teacher, then be one that truly inspires. If you're a preacher, then be the best damn preacher you can be. And if you fail, who cares? At least you went down swinging. Besides, your salvation does not hang in the balance. Your eternity is not fashioned by your own hands. Only the blood of the Lamb decided that. You are saved by grace alone, so you are free to work, free to fail, and free to get up again and again.

So get out the tool box, roll up your sleeves, and do the work our Lord has given you to do.

OLD BOOKS AND NEW PULPITS

PAUL KOCH

Right before I left seminary for the parish, I happily spent some time with Dr. Feuerhahn before hitting the road. I remember him generously unloading some of his excess library from his study onto me. This was his response to me mentioning that one of my great fears about leaving the seminary was leaving behind its incredible library.

I loved the library. I still like to wander through it when I get a chance to go back. The library held the promise of answers and guidance for my vocation as a pastor.

I loved the smell of the old books and marveled at the massive collection of great theologians, past and present. I could get lost in the stacks below for hours and be quite happy. From ancient texts to contemporary journal articles, the library was a powerful tool to any who sought to be a preacher of the word. Leaving such a treasure trove behind was a bit scary. It was like taking off the training wheels the day before a big race. The tools of the library would surely aid me in being a better preacher, so I was shaky about leaving it behind.

Dr. Feuerhahn said that when he visits pastors in the parish, he can often tell what year they graduated simply by looking at their library. His point was that there are often no new books purchased after graduation. The personal libraries of many pastors look like snapshots of the curriculum's required reading for whatever period of time they were at the seminary.

Now, with the accessibility of the Internet and the great amount of quality materials in digital form, his point may seem a little dated, but his sentiment is quite true. At least when it comes to the task of striving to be better preachers, most pastors' libraries haven't changed much. A great danger facing many of us pastors is that we are lazy. Now, please understand. I'm not saying that they aren't busy. Most pastors are swamped, but they tend to be lazy in regards to bettering themselves in their task as preachers.

The vast majority of conversations I have had with my colleagues in the pastoral ministry deal with practicalities. Our discussions deal with stewardship, youth ministry, confirmation, evangelism, mission strategy, and the like. More often, they are concerned with particular issues with particular members. Sometimes we will even argue doctrinal distinctions and exegetical struggles in a particular text. But it is rare when the discussion turns to the task of preaching. The quest to be better preachers seems to be low on the agenda. This point is proven by the schedule for almost every pastors' conference I've ever been to.

It's time for preachers to dust off the old books and buy some new ones. It's time to reclaim the craft of preaching. It's time for preaching to move to the top of our agendas!

I leave you with this quote from C. F. W. Walther:

How pitiful is the young pastor who enters this office thinking: "Hooray, the time of hard work and drudgery is over. Now I have come to the haven of rest and peace! I will enjoy that! I am my own boss and need not take orders from any person in the world!" This is just as pitiful s the pastor who looks upon his office as his craft, or trade, and thinks: "Now all I have to do is to set up for myself a nice, comfortable parish! I will be really careful not to make enemies and do everything to make everyone my friend." Oh, what a pitiful man! These pastors plan to use their spiritual assets for worldly gain. They are not true ministers of Christ, and on the Last Day He will say to them, "I never knew you; depart from Me, you workers of lawlessness" (Matt. 7:23).

But blessed is the pastor who starts his official work on the very first day, determined to do everything that the grace of God will enable him to do, so that not one soul in his congregation would be lost on account of him. A pastor like this would resolve that by the grace of God he would do all he can, so that, when the day comes for him to lay down his shepherd's staff, he may be able to say what Christ said to His Father, "Here I am. Of those You gave me, not one is lost." (Walther, Law and Gospel, *"Twentieth Evening Lecture")*

THE GRANITE NEVER LIES

PAUL KOCH

My wife and I took a trip to Yosemite National Park with our good friends Scott and Joy. We wanted to make a break for it and get to the mountains. Within six hours, we found ourselves standing at the trailhead that leads to Upper Yosemite Falls. While I would love to try to explain the grandeur and awe-inspiring vistas of such a journey, that is not really my point, nor do I think I could capture such beauty in words. Rather, what I want to share is how crucial such tasks are in our lives.

The trail to the top of the falls is three-and-a-half miles long and covers roughly 2,700 feet of elevation gain. I'm not going to lie. It was a difficult climb with more switchbacks than I care to remember, and that was the blessing. It wasn't a shifting scene where "good enough" was going to cut it or you could BS your way through. It was a trail cut into a granite mountain that you were going to either conquer or lose to; there was no gray area.

Too often in our lives, we spend our time never having to deal with an objective and immovable measure of our strength and resolve. We wander around from one situation to another always ready with excuses and rhetoric to shape the stories that make us look good, stroke our own egos, or explain away our failures.

Henry Rollins expressed a similar sentiment when discussing the realities of lifting weights in a now famous essay titled "Iron and the Soul." Rollins says:

> *The Iron never lies to you. You can walk outside and listen to all kinds of talk, get told that you're a god or a total bastard. The Iron will always kick you the real deal. The Iron is the great reference point, the all-knowing perspective giver. Always there like a beacon in the pitch black. I have found the Iron to be my greatest friend. It never freaks out on me, never runs. Friends may come and go. But two hundred pounds is always two hundred pounds.*

The thing is, if we only spend our time as victors in the electronic world of video games, or consume our days in eloquent discussions with disembodied "friends" on Facebook, or only execute academic arguments that don't come crashing into the lives of people around us, then we will never know who we really are. Without an objective measure outside of ourselves, how can we ever know if our ideas really matter, or if we can be of service to others, or if we can overcome?

Get outside. Get to the gym. Get on a bike. Lace up your running shoes. Do something that won't allow you to lie to yourself. It's OK to fail, at least then you know where you really stand!

PART THREE
FAMILY

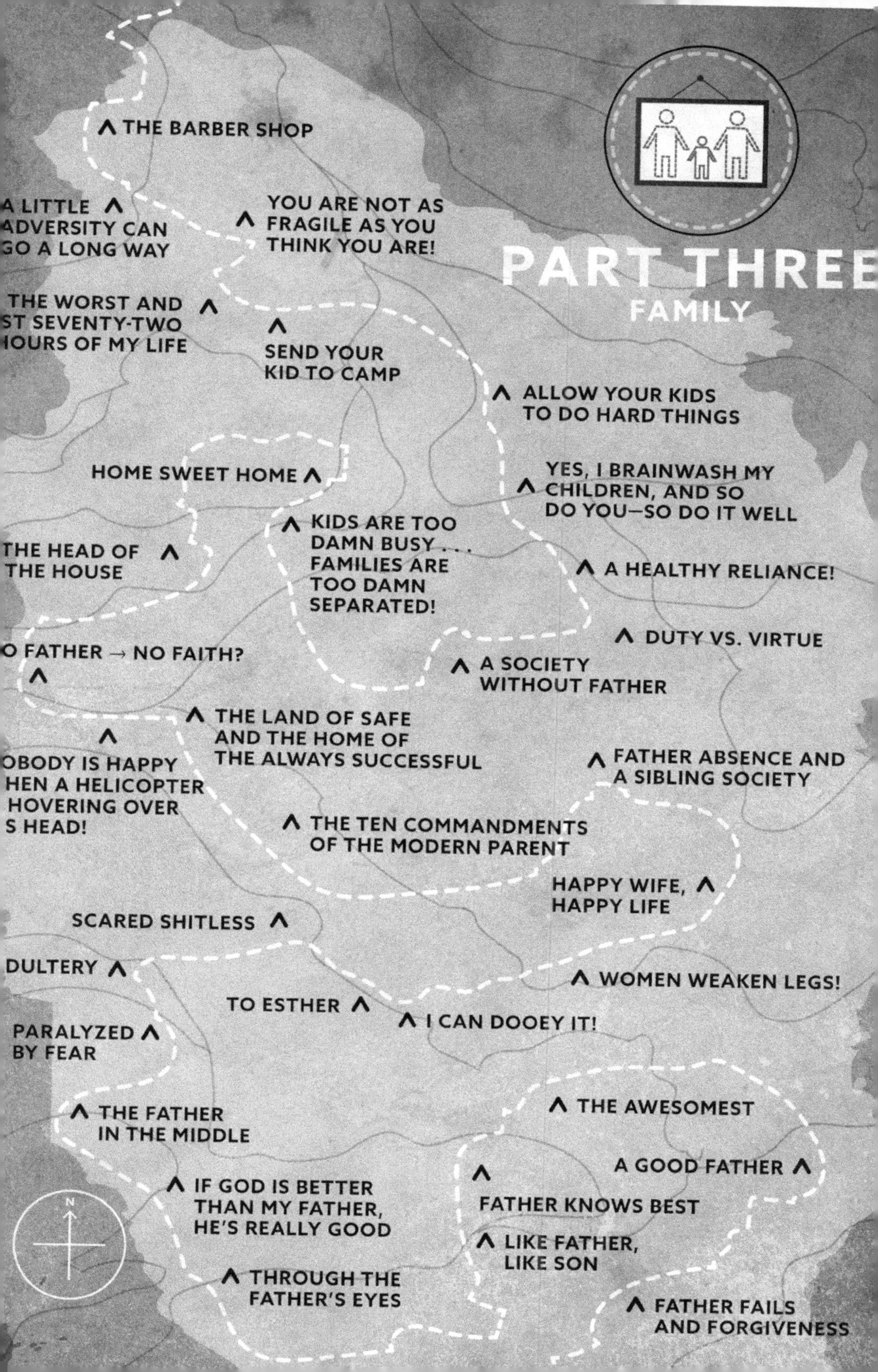

THE BARBER SHOP

PAUL KOCH

When it's haircut day for my son, I usually break out the clippers to do it myself. But I had great joy when I took him to my barber to have his hair done right by a man who knows what he's doing. Something about the crude conversation among those happy to be involved creates a beauty to the barbershop that I can't quite describe, and I love that I get to experience it with my son.

The barber set him up on the booster seat; other than that one piece of furniture, he was treated like any other man in the joint. Now, being only four years old, it was a lot of work for Titus to sit still for that long. He managed quite well while engulfed in adult conversation, either being the butt of the jokes or being asked to help make fun of the guys cutting hair next to him. It was good for him to experience this, to soak in the atmosphere, even if he was just thinking about the ice cream I promised him afterward.

As I look at my son, I am filled with pride and hopefulness. I might well fear for a boy growing up in a world that has embraced the role of men as narcissistic metrosexuals or overly trendy hipsters—but I don't. Much of what passes for manhood these days holds no sway over the character of a true man, and the shaping of that character lies not in the whims of a consumerist society but in the actions and words of his father.

I have five children, and my son is the youngest. Correct, he has four older sisters! While he has certainly learned how to use them and their motherly instincts to his advantage, he has also learned about restraint and patience. He has learned not to hit a girl, no matter how much they might deserve it. He has learned the importance of holding the door open for the ladies of the house before entering himself. He has watched me love and care for his mother and all his sisters. While I have certainly made many mistakes, he is still learning to be a man.

You see, I believe that I am the single biggest influence upon my son's life. The man he will become, his character and resolve, will be a byproduct of my own character—my own interactions with those around us and my own treatment of those who need to be cared for, welcomed, or forgiven.

I'm saying that I expect my son to be a man of integrity and resolve. I expect him to interact with this world and hold his own. I expect him to treat his future wife with honor and respect. And as silly as it may sound, sometimes that begins with a trip to the barbershop to practice the things of manhood and to come home with our heads held high and our bellies full of ice cream.

A LITTLE ADVERSITY CAN GO A LONG WAY

SCOTT KEITH

Our culture is reticent to allow any discomfort or pain to enter our lives. It seems that people don't have the same capacity to bounce back as history tells us they once did. Resiliency is a lost art that we seemingly hope will stay lost. Pain, while contrary to God's original plan for His creation, is nonetheless a reality of life in the fallen world. I am no more masochistic than the next guy and do not think that we ought to actively seek pain or adversity. Yet we cannot daily act as if pain can be utterly avoided. Further, we ought to allow our children to encounter pain and adversity time and again before they leave the protection of our nests so that they are familiar with it when they face it in the world—and they will.

I love to go camping. Camping, to one degree or another, has been a part of our family life for some twenty years. I love that it reminds me of the reality of my comfortable life, as it is a little hard. When I camp with my wife, we sleep on the ground and cook food over a fire. We are hot when it's hot outside and cold when it's cold outside. Our world is real in these moments.

Sometimes it sucks. Just ask my wife about our camping trip to the Grand Canyon when we woke up to a morning that was a shocking 7°F. It is always real, authentic hard work. Camping makes me reminisce of a time when cooking, gathering water, and trying to occasionally be comfortable were the norm and not the exception. Now we are completely content and comfortable all the time. When I come back from a camping trip, I always appreciate my soft bed and the free-flowing water from the various sinks and showers in our apartment.

Before you accuse me of being an overly nostalgic cultural critic who wishes he lived a hundred years ago, try to understand the core of what I am saying. The truth is, I like penicillin as much as the next guy when I have strep throat. And I love the MacBook Air on which I write this blog. I don't want to be teleported back to 1914. Rather, I appreciate the fact that adversity produces character, and I abhor the fact that adversity is avoided at all costs in our society. I often feel as though we fear being scared and we fear at all levels that our children will one day get hurt, be told no, or have to solve a problem on their own—God forbid.

A *Forbes* article that circulated on Facebook listed seven crippling parenting behaviors that severely limit children's potential growth. I won't rephrase the article word for word, but just look at the list: (1) We don't let our children experience risk, (2) we rescue them too quickly, (3) we rave too easily, (4) we let guilt get in the way of leading well, (5) we don't share our past mistakes, (6) we mistake intelligence, giftedness, and influence for maturity, and (7) we don't practice what we preach. When are we going to realize that the practices of sheltering and overpraising just don't work?

Let's flip the list around to see what we should do. First, we need to let our children experience risk. Let them do things that might result in a broken arm, a dental appointment, stitches, or even hurt feelings. Second, we don't need to rescue our children every time they are in trouble. Rather, we need to let them face their own adversity and figure out their own solutions. Not every adversity is going to scar our children for life. In fact, facing difficulty will likely make them better people. Third, our children are not all the most special children on the planet, and we need to stop telling them they are. They are poor, miserable sinners like the rest of us and need to know that they are forgiven in Christ as well. Perfect people have no need for a Christ who saves sinners. Personally, I want my children to know that Christ died for their sins, which are abundant. Fourth, we need to stop allowing guilt and fear to determine how we act and raise our children. Decisions made because of guilt and fear, especially parenting decisions, will only result in the negative outcomes we seek to avoid. Fifth, we need to let our children know that we are not perfect by sharing with them the mistakes we have made and what we have learned from those mistakes. Sixth, maturity comes from overcoming adversity.

If we don't allow our children to personally experience adversity, no matter how intelligent or "gifted" they are, they will never become mature. So allow them to experience and overcome adversity at appropriate levels. Lastly, we need to stop being hypocrites. If we expect hard work, we need to model hard work. If we expect maturity, we need to model maturity. If we think that facing adversity develops maturity, then we need to face and overcome it ourselves. We need to experience discomfort with our families now and again so that they can identify it and know how to overcome it. We need to take our children camping, let them get jobs, do chores and yard work, help us fix the car, and all the other sometimes uncomfortable adversities that help all of us truly become mature, resilient, and productive members of society. Remember, a little adversity can go a long way.

YOU ARE NOT AS FRAGILE AS YOU THINK YOU ARE!

SCOTT KEITH

About twelve times a day, I feel like screaming the title of this entry from the rooftops. How did we in the United States, supposedly the greatest country in the world, come to believe that we are so fragile? We were the country that tamed the West, led the Industrial Revolution, built the greatest infrastructure known in human history, saved Europe during two World Wars, and beat the Soviet Union in the Cold War—and now we feel as though we'll die if our house only has two bathrooms. Now we want everything to be given to us already bigger and better without having to make it so. We want the result without any of the work. We want the easy without the hard. Where have we gone so wrong? I have come to believe that it is the hard things that make life worth living. In embracing this, I have had to embrace the reality that I am not as physically, spiritually, or emotionally fragile as I think I am. Neither are you.

Without making this about living simply, I want to say that I think that we have it too easy in America. We seem to believe that suffering means that our children share a bedroom in our

1,500-square-foot house. We seem to believe that it would be impossible for anyone, especially ourselves, to endure the temporary loss of a meal, electricity, indoor plumbing, a soft bed, the Internet, TV, or Starbucks for even a day. Yet many people all over the world see these things as luxuries, not as necessities, and manage to do without them every day. They are not as fragile as you think they are. Neither are you.

My wife and I took a two-day trip to Yosemite with my friend Paul and his wife, Cindy. This trip was not one in which we "roughed it" by any stretch of the imagination. In fact, we stayed in a nice B&B about fifty minutes outside of the park. Yet the trip was fraught with some tough adventures that made all of us realize that we aren't as fragile as we think we are. We hiked to the top of Yosemite Falls, which was hard for some of us physically, mentally, and spiritually. The hike was difficult; we were short on water, the landscape was inspiring yet demanding, and we were all at different levels of ability to complete the task. Seven hours later, we made it up and down, sore and thirsty, but safe and sound nonetheless. You see, we were not as fragile as we thought we were. Neither are you.

I have enjoyed spending time in the outdoors since I was a teenager. I have never quite understood exactly why because I am not one who appreciates beauty as much as I should. I love living simply, but I don't think that sums it up either.

Recently, I have come to think that we have it easy in day-to-day life. Sometimes it feels right to do something hard, whether it is a tough hike, a grueling mountain bike ride, an arduous trail run, or a nearly impossible climb. Hard tasks encourage me to stop lying to myself. I like it when a rock or a trail reminds me of how limited I really am. When I know my limits, I know that I was created very well. Yet I am a sinner who still has the *imago Dei* within me, and I am not as fragile as I think I am. Neither are you. Not to be too cliché with the proof texts, but the apostle Paul said something similar: "And not only this, but we also exult in our tribulations, knowing that tribulation brings about perseverance; and perseverance, proven character; and proven character, hope; and hope does not disappoint, because the love of God has been poured out within our hearts through the Holy Spirit who was given to us" (Rom. 5:3). Go do something hard that will allow you to stop lying to yourself for a day. Make your kids do some hard stuff before they leave the nest. The rest of the world will thank you for it. Let's all gain a little more "proven character" when we can.

THE WORST AND BEST SEVENTY-TWO HOURS OF MY LIFE

GRAHAM GLOVER

I will never forget the day my daughter was born. Being our first child, her birthday was, at that point, the single best day of my life. (I say this with all due apologies to my wife and our glorious wedding day, but I think she agrees with me.)

I was simply overwhelmed when our daughter was born. As is the case with many first-time parents, I was elated—even if a bit frightened about what being a father is all about. Holding her for the first time, I remember asking myself, "Am I a father?" The emotions were incredible. That day was pure joy.

But less than seventy-two hours earlier, my world was turned upside down by the single worst day of my life. Sitting at my desk writing my sermon for the following Sunday, I received a call from my great-aunt telling me that my father was dead. His death was completely unexpected. He had just walked my sister down the aisle a couple of weeks earlier. My body went numb upon hearing the news before I let out a scream that caused my eight-and-a-half-months pregnant wife to come running to my office. My grandmother took the phone from her sister, and together we cried as she grieved the loss of her only living child and me the loss of my dad.

To say that my emotions were all over the place that first week of May 2005 would be the understatement of my life. I cried a lot, never sure if I was happy or sad. The pain of death and the glory of life were on full display for my family and me. One minute I was filled with a joy I had never known, completely delighted, and the next I was heartbroken, utterly devastated. It was, without question, the worst and best seventy-two hours of my life.

Ten years later, I still remember that week as if it was yesterday. There isn't a day gone by that I have not mourned my father, nor given thanks for the life of my daughter, as well as my wife, son, mother, and siblings. I still miss my dad a lot. From time to time, there are still tears and some very raw emotions.

But mine is not a unique experience. Most of us have seen death. We have been confronted with its pain up close and personally. This is the tragedy of our fallen, sinful world; our bodies are not perfect. They will ultimately fail, and we will all die. A baptized child of God, he is among the communion of the saints, but my father was no saint. He was a wretched sinner whose shortcomings I knew all too well. He loved the Lord and sought comfort in His word and sacraments, but my dad—like each of us—was never going to live forever.

All of us will die—some sooner than expected. But die we shall; this much is certain. All of us will experience death, including those closest to us. We will feel its sting and cry out in pain. There are no simple words, no Hallmark clichés, that can take the horror of death away. It is sure to come. And it sucks. It really, really sucks. For ten years I have suffered its consequences, and I hate it today as much as I ever have.

Death, however, has no mastery over me. It may poke, prod, and rear its ugly head. I will succumb to it one day and those I love dearest will as well. But death will not win. As often as

I experience it, as many times as I see and feel it, I will always find comfort in a joy that is far greater than death.

I say these things confidently, without any hesitation, because, in this glorious Easter season, I know that my Redeemer lives. Christ is risen! He is risen from the dead. Death has no mastery over Him or any who are part of His kingdom. I am at peace in my Savior, who has forgiven me, as he has my father and my daughter. He has won eternal life for us, as He has for you. He has defeated death. He has conquered it—once for all—and in so doing, He offers the joy of life with Him forever.

My father is dead, but one day he will rise with the Lord. My daughter is ten, and when this same Lord returns, she will be reunited with her grandfather. To God alone be the glory!

SEND YOUR
KID TO CAMP

GRAHAM GLOVER

I'm not one for self-help books. You know the volumes that fill every bookstore, promising success with their seven-step models. These books are often garbage and a waste of your resources and time.

I'm also not the best parent. I like to think that I'm a decent dad (my Father's Day cards tell me I am the best), but I've got a lot of work to do (just don't tell my kids).

But hear me loud and clear: *send your kids to camp!* It is the best thing they can do during the summer. If you can, send them to more than one. Ideally, send them to an overnight camp. Make it at least a week long; two weeks would be better. A month would be incredible. But send them. Send them until they can become a counselor, and then encourage them to do so. Why? Summer camp is the greatest thing a kid can do.

I'm not pushing any one camp or camp style. All boys, all girls, or coed; secular or religious; sports-focused or fun-focused; north, south, east, or west—it doesn't matter. The key is to get kids out of the house, away from their parents, in a new environment, and in a place where they will be challenged, have fun, and appreciate what it means to be a kid.

My camp alma mater (five years as a camper and five as a counselor), Camp Crystal Lake, is a place to which I would return in a heartbeat. Those ten summers were some of the best and most formative of my life. I'm thrilled that my daughter attends the camp too. There's even a rumor that some of us counselors might have a reunion sometime soon.

At camp, a child learns to appreciate the wonders of the outdoors. Even if they already spend a lot of time outside, camp has a way of reinforcing the true joy of getting away from iPods, TVs, computers, and other screens. Too many of the privates I see in basic training have no idea how to function outside—physically or emotionally. A good camp is focused almost entirely on being outside—the place we humans are most naturally situated and where we have the most fun.

At camp, a child is challenged with people, obstacles, activities, and counselors that are often different from what they experience during the school year. These challenges can do more to mature and teach a child than months of instruction in a classroom. Adults know that life isn't easy and that failures confront us time and again. Yet we persevere in living through our respective vocations. Camp teaches these important life lessons, even if kids don't realize it at the time. In teaching children these lessons, they become better students, athletes, and kids. I'm a staunch traditionalist, but I love the idea that camp can destroy stereotypes and give different perspectives to presuppositions about life.

I was well rooted in my faith and my family, but the people I met as a camper and counselor showed me that there is a big world out there, with lots of different ways of living and many diverse ideas on things. This shouldn't scare parents but excite them. Summer camp can be the linchpin for discussions and growth that would have taken years to begin without it.

Camp can also be the greatest tool in teaching children independence. Overnight camp does this best. The longer they are away, the more independent they become. Sure, you can keep your child within the safety bubble of their home and neighborhood, where everything is as planned to be. Or they can go to a camp where they learn and grow with challenging activities and interesting, eclectic campers/counselors. Children can become either hermits or people who can function outside the safe and comfortable confines of home.

Oh, to be a child again. Oh, to be a camper.

Get with it, parents. Send your kids to camp!

ALLOW YOUR KIDS TO DO HARD THINGS

SCOTT KEITH

This is a bit of a rehash and more than a slight piggyback on Graham's plea for you to send your kids to camp. What can I say? I was inspired by what he wrote. I also went to camp from the time I was eight years old, through my preteen years, into my teen years. I became a CIT (counselor-in-training) and a lifeguard. Eventually, I worked as a camp counselor, program director, and director. Camp is in my blood. There are many things I learned from going to camp, but I especially learned from working there. Mostly, what I learned was the importance of doing hard things. Be it simply living on your own for a bit, building a fire, clearing a trail, splitting wood, building retaining walls, mopping floors, or cleaning toilets, working at camp can be hard.

Our culture seems to encourage us to avoid these hard tasks. Our culture discourages people from learning services skills and manual labor trades and promotes any kind of office work over manual labor. In other words, avoid what is hard and seek that which brings the largest payoff for the least amount of physical or emotional effort. It is not my place to tell anyone what they should do when they "grow up." Nonetheless, I do know that if children are not encouraged to do hard things when they are young, then life—which is hard—will be a big surprise to them when they are grown.

The Keith family has changed a lot, which is hard—but hard is good. Our oldest son, Caleb, got married. Our second son, Joshua, left home to work in a glass shop and learn a trade that will stick with him for the rest of his life. And finally, our daughter Autumn, our youngest, went to stay with her brother, attending the camp where he works. As they learned hard lessons, Joy and I learned what married life is like without them around. The process of letting them go has been scary. Our culture says that Caleb is too young to get married. Joshua is too young to have a full-time manual labor job. Our culture is wrong.

Current research seems to point to the disappointing reality that people do not reach what would be considered mental adulthood until their mid-to-late twenties. Why is that the case? Perhaps it's because their parents are so terrified that they may come to some harm that we don't allow them to do hard things while they are young. Encountering hard things and overcoming them are what make a person mature. Maturity is not defined by age; it is defined by how we act when it matters.

Yet doing what is needed in the face of adversity takes quite a bit of practice and often seems like a long journey. This journey feels so long that we are hesitant to let our children start it at all. Every day we delay from allowing them to take that first step—walking themselves to school, getting their first job, leaving home for extended periods of time—the longer it will take to complete the trip. Let's all get our kids to take those first steps by allowing them to do something hard today.

YES, I BRAINWASH MY CHILDREN, AND SO DO YOU— SO DO IT WELL

JOEL HESS

Time and time again, I hear friends say with complete sincerity, "I don't want to force my kids to go to church," or "I want my kids to choose what they want to believe in." They brag about it as if it's a badge of honor and an enlightened sign of good parenting.

We flippantly believe that we live in a postmodern age, yet this common attitude among Generation X parents has more in common with the modern or even early Enlightenment Age than Nietzsche or Warhol. Contrary to what some knee-jerk conservatives preach, the postmodern age has blessed our culture with a couple of timeless truths (yes, I recognize the ironic juxtaposition of "truth" and "postmodern"). One mantra of postmodernism is that it is impossible not to be brainwashed in our culture. It is impossible not to have or receive biases from parents. Everything parents say or do, or don't say or do, fills their little sponges with biases. Ugh!

By not making their kids go to church, let alone failing to teach them the faith, parents are teaching them something quite clear about the church and Christianity. Even if a mom teaches her child about every religion in the world and concludes, "You make a choice," she is catechizing her student. One might even say that a parent is forcing their child not to be a Christian by allowing them to "make their own choice."

I praise God every day. I was given no choice in the matter! Instead, God chose me, forgiving my sins, giving me new life, freeing me of the old, and yes, brainwashing me to see things as He sees them.

In the end, we are all brainwashed. Whether purposely or inadvertently, all flesh is catechized. We are not born blank slates, contrary to the cute meme out there portraying two toddlers of different races hugging with the caption, "Hate is taught." Yeah, right. Have you ever hung out with more than one toddler?

We are born with darkened, hell-bent souls, brains, and hearts. That's not just from Holy Scripture but from science as well. No child looks at the world from some blessed neutrality. Our instincts repel against love, peace, and God. All of us, from Mother Teresa to St. Paul, were born haters of Christianity. We needed our brains washed and freed by Christ through His church.

Everyone has been brainwashed and taught about life, about God. All people from every tribe, ethnicity, and language are militantly catechized by someone in one way or another. The difference is who did the brainwashing. Was it the one who died and rose again? Or was it someone with less stellar credentials?

Sadly, many Christian parents don't quite get it. Yes, they bring their kids to church services. Great! They bring them to extra events such as youth group and confirmation class. Fantastic! God does what He wills through His word—period!

However, parents forget that they are an important part of the brainwashing. No, they don't have to do it all. However, by not teaching their kids the faith at home, even a simple devotion and prayer, they are teaching their kids something about the faith: it only matters in a particular place and time. They will learn that only pastors are supposed to take Christ and His gifts seriously. They will learn that in the "real" world, Jesus is just a spectator. They will learn from their parents the opposite of what they learn from Jesus. They may grow up and say, "My parents forced me to go to church, so I don't go now." They will say that because the Christian faith felt like a place they must go to instead of a reality in which Mom and Dad clung to Christ every day. It isn't universities or TV that are primarily causing twentysomethings to leave the church; it is parents who fail to teach their kids or even let them see the real-life meaning of the forgiveness of sins, the resurrection, and a God who loves them.

Yes, I brainwash my kids. So do you. Do it well.

A HEALTHY RELIANCE!

SCOTT KEITH

Disclaimer: I am not a clinical or any other type of psychologist, nor do I claim to have any expertise in that field. I am a husband, parent, college professor, and theologian who, like my mentor Dr. Rod Rosenbladt, is interested in the intersection between the theology of the Reformation and fatherhood. I am not an expert, just a thinker.

s there a difference between a healthy and an unhealthy reliance? I wrote a blog for the *1517 Legacy Project* called "On Being a Dad—a Tribute to Dr. Rod Rosenbladt." This was a difficult thing to write and consumed much of my mental energy after its posting. As I have ruminated on this topic, it has become clear to me that possessing a view of fathers such as mine—that they are the models of grace in the home—creates a reliance in my children on me that seems endless and unbounded. This reality scares me. I am the original criticizer of helicopter and snowplow parents, and I wonder if I am just that.

I once had a conversation with Rod about this when I was a much younger man with much younger children. He told me that he had received criticism from a friend saying that his children were too reliant on him, to which he retorted, "Maybe, but it's a healthy reliance." This statement from Rod caused me to think: What does a healthy reliance from a grown child to a parent or parents look like? In my position at the university, I see many parent–grown child relationships that seem unhealthy. I could recognize this unhealthy reliance from a mile away, but a healthy one seems a little vaguer to me.

Ironically, in my world, this seems to be a pretty hot topic. The last time I was together with my friends Paul and Cindy Koch, we discussed this same topic. How much reliance from a grown child to a parent is too much reliance? Perhaps the best way to approach this is to break the question down into its pieces and examine each situation. By doing this, we can compare unhealthy reliance and healthy reliance.

From what I have observed, unhealthy reliances share some common behaviors. First, when parents foster an unhealthy reliance, they seem to be afraid to allow their children to get hurt, experience loss, fail, or go through situations that are extremely difficult. Second, parents in this relationship seem to be afraid to say "no" ever, for fear that their children will no longer love them. These same parents seem to be willing to sacrifice everything while refusing to allow their grown children to sacrifice anything. In turn, the grown children seem to see these sacrifices on the part of their parents as privileges to which they are entitled; these are perks of being lucky enough to be born of their parents.

On the other hand, a healthy reliance is still a very giving relationship, but it is gracious, not smothering. A healthy reliance does not hide from the fact that children—even grown children—are sinners and will at times get hurt, experience loss, failure, and go through extremely difficult life situations. In turn, because a relationship of healthy reliance does not hide from this reality, parents will allow their children to experience those very difficult aspects of living in a sinful world. But because a healthy reliance is gracious, it will not bring unyielding condemnation or sanctimony down on grown children when they experience failure but will help them to pick up the pieces. The pieces can be picked up in many ways (I would not presume to know what is best for you or your family in any particular situation) but will always set the grown child free to make the same damn mistakes again. The theme here is grace and freedom.

How many times will a grown child fail before we stop helping them? I'm not sure, but I know that if their reliance is on our love for them, the grace that we show to them and the freedom with which we trust them, we are on the right track. If Rod is an example, and he has been for me, a healthy reliance is about grace, love, trust, freedom, and mercy. These are characteristics Christians, should already be familiar. Those of us who know we are helpless sinners in need of a gracious Father to save us on account of His mercy shown to us in Christ will know that we parents have no greater example. We are shadows, imperfect reflections, of his love for us, but we are shadows of this love nonetheless. We rely on His love for us because of Christ, and from the outside looking in that probably looks unhealthy. But we who are bathed in Christ's love know that there is no healthier reliance that we could ever dream to find. My goal is to be a shadow of that healthy reliance as I forge this new relationship with my growing, and grown children.

DUTY VS. VIRTUE

SCOTT KEITH

s it every parent's duty to send his or her child to college? Is it the duty of every high school student to go to college after graduation? I recently moderated a discussion in one of my freshman seminar sections in which I asked the students to reflect upon their motivations for attending college. I was surprised to hear that most noted that they came to college because they "had to." Since I have always viewed post–high school education as a privilege and in many cases even a luxury, this was perplexing to me. Because it is a privilege, I have always taught my children that they should go to college if they want the education. Once there, I have asked them to seek out every educational opportunity possible. What was even more perplexing in this discussion was that some of these same students desired to serve in careers that didn't necessarily require a college diploma. $20,000 to $40,000 a year is quite costly if one is not attending college for the vast educational opportunities available at most four-year institutions of higher education. It's even more costly if the degree being sought is not needed for one's desired vocational pursuits.

I believe that these students feel a sense of duty to attend college because their parents, as well as society, have led them to believe that they need a degree to succeed. Many blogs, articles, and books have been written that have completely debunked the idea that it is necessary to obtain a college degree to have a good career in America and be happy. If anyone would like a primer on this, feel free to Google the *TED Talks* lecture delivered by Mike Rowe. Better yet, read Matthew B. Crawford's *Shop Class as Soul Craft*. But even if Mike and Matthew are wrong, is a sense of duty why people ought to attend university? I think not.

The classic liberal arts education was designed to educate free people to think freely. As such, it focused on virtue rather than duty. It is virtuous for a university to offer a variety of fields of study and for students to want to learn from them. Science, mathematics, history, literature, philosophy, and even theology are valuable subjects capable of developing those who study them into well-rounded and virtuous people who can contribute freely to society. Fulfilling one's duty rarely produces a desire to use what has been learned to contribute in a virtuous way to the world around us. Freedom to learn produces a desire to learn. A desire to learn produces a desire to apply what one has learned in a positive, contributive way. At Concordia University Irvine, we often say that we are developing wise, honorable, and cultivated citizens for lives of learning and service. Virtue emphasizes one's developed character and freedom to serve neighbors, while duty emphasizes only adherence to perceived cultural rules or norms.

Students should invest in education for the sake of becoming educated. To become educated is the virtuous option. I believe it is those who are well educated who discover what virtue has meant throughout time. It is they who are likely to become virtuous themselves. I also believe that education can be had in the classroom, in the workshop, or in the home. But nonetheless, everyone ought to become exceedingly educated in his or her field. Pursue education and learning in all their forms, desire virtue over duty, and find virtue in your calling. In the world of duty vs. virtue, virtue ought to win because it's born of freedom, not bondage, and is what produces wise, honorable, and cultivated citizens. If you send your child to college, send them to be educated. Encourage them to seek and pursue every educational opportunity in whatever it is God has called them to be so that they learn to master their field and find virtue in their service to others.

A SOCIETY
WITHOUT FATHER

SCOTT KEITH

I've done a fair amount of research on the subject of fatherhood. I'm interested in answering a couple of questions:
(1) "What makes a good father?" and (2) "What impact does
a good father have on the lives of his children?" As I survey our
society, it seems that we live contentedly in a world without
fathers. This will have long-lasting implications for our children
and our culture. As a part of my research, I looked to Alexander Mitscherlich's *Society without the Father*. Mitscherlich was a
social psychologist in post–World War II Germany. In his society,
he saw that fathers were absent and prophetically noted that
America was the next society to abandon and marginalize the
father. Having said that, please note that nothing that I write for
you today is original. The few insights that I share with you here
are Mitscherlich's insights as I have adapted them in a simplistic
format.

The father in our world is absent, first because he is gone all
day at work, out of the sight of his children, and second because
society marginalizes and mocks his role in the family. Now, it's
not that we can go back to a preindustrial lifestyle or even that
anyone in our iPhone world would want to, but some things in

our past ought to be remembered. One of the important realities to remember is that no matter what the mood in the homes of the past might have been, the life of the parents—Father included—took place before the eyes of the children. Further, what he contributed was physically and emotionally necessary. No important aspect of adult life would have taken place outside of the children's sight or, for that matter, would have been beyond their range of experience. In our world, the father leaves at 6 or 7 a.m. and returns at 5 or 6 p.m. The net result is that the father, when he does make an appearance, is a striking figure. Further, if Mother uses him as the heavy in a "wait-till-your-father-gets-home" way, he is a terror-striking figure. Or the modern father may choose to be a passive and invisible figure even at home. Our world seems to desire them to be just that. Father doesn't know best; that's up to Mother.

Rivalry between a father and his children, particularly his sons, is natural. In the old world, these rivalries were sorted out nonverbally by working together toward a goal that benefited the whole family. The son could build a fence with his father. By doing this, he shows his skills that he learned from his father. They would compete, but in a way that was helpful to their relationship, not harmful. The competition would relieve the tension between father and son. The tension did not need expressing. It did not result in verbal or physical fighting. It was released in the accomplishing of a task together.

There is little or no working alongside the father to relieve tension nowadays; there is only the building of tension and confusion. His life does not occur before the eyes of his children, nor theirs in front of his. They do not see what he does, and he does not see what they are learning. The comingling of the father as a whole person—his temperament and his roles as mentor, teacher, provider, caregiver, and friend—has been put aside. The father as his temperament remains at the end of the day, but the father in all other forms seems distant. At the risk of sounding sanctimonious, this is one of the primary reasons to homeschool children. The process of homeschooling usually requires Father to be involved in some way in the teaching process. Father and Mother must work together to cover the whole gamut of subjects and skills necessary to the educational process. Be it leaving work early or taking every other Friday to teach science, Father usually needs to be more involved than less.

Now, certainly more needs to be said than this oversimplified word. But perhaps a few takeaways can be noted. First, be more than your temperament to your children. Do what you can to be all aspects of a father. They need your teaching, care, deep instruction, grace, presence, guidance, and mentorship; they need it all. Also, show them what you do at work and teach them about it. Don't hide your work world from your children. Teach them to be proud and interested in the whole you. You are not two people. You are one person, their father. They want to know the whole you and they want to learn from you about that part of your life that you spend away from them for forty to sixty hours per week. Lastly, see your callings as a husband and a father as your primary earthly callings. What you do at work is done to support them, but without the total you as the father in their life, what you do at work is of less value to them than you might think. Be more than the monetary and physical support to them; be their dad. We need to stop accepting a society without fathers or with a distant fathers and start demanding a society with fathers. Please pray for me as I daily attempt to take my own advice, and I'll do the same for you.

KIDS ARE TOO DAMN BUSY . . . FAMILIES ARE TOO DAMN SEPARATED!

SCOTT KEITH

Has anyone else noticed that our family lives are ridiculous? Our children have commitments that extend late into the night on Saturday and even Sunday. It seems like we need to readjust what we ask our children to do and why we ask them to do it. In 2004, a Roper Poll found that on average, children between the ages of five and eighteen spent about five hours per week in organized activities—about the same amount of time they spent in out-of-school educational activities ("Public Agenda Foundation Poll"). This same poll indicated that these children seldom felt as though it was parental pressure nudging them forward to participate. This doesn't seem too bad, but I wonder, what aren't they spending time doing? In other words, how much time per week is spent as a family, with parents, not practicing the flute or soccer but just learning to be part of a family? As a case in point, this same poll found that these children spent less time performing household chores and hanging out with their family and more time playing video games and watching television. Keep in mind that for a family with three children, this will mean that fifteen hours per week of lost family time will be spent chasing children around from event to event. This doesn't even count the commute time.

Now, I do not intend to portray participation in sports or music lessons as evil. Rather, I want to understand what we hope to accomplish culturally by asking most of our children to spend a greater amount of time learning to be the next great baseball player or flautist than learning how to function in a family. Athletics will keep our children fit and healthy. That is a good thing. Musical training can help with academics, memorization, and mathematical ability. These too are good things. Learning to be part of a family means doing chores, socializing with one another, cooking, playing games, supporting those you love, and caring for common possessions and values. These are great things. In fact, these are the things that hold societies together and have held them together since the beginning of recorded history. Yet we ask our children to spend less than five hours a week in this arena and more than five hours a week learning to throw a ball through a hoop.

Further, this survey can claim that parents do not put pressure on their children to be in these activities, but I think that is a load of crap. I think the parents who were surveyed sugarcoated the reality. I can't be the only one that time and again must listen to some idiotic parent droning on about how their child needs to succeed in swimming, volleyball, or softball so that they can get the all-important scholarship for their bachelor's degree to be all they can be in life. Newsflash, less than 2 percent of undergraduate students are awarded athletic scholarships. On the other hand, around 40 percent of students receive some sort of merit or academic-based scholarship. So if you want your child to do well in college and receive some help paying for it, keep them home and help them with their homework rather than insisting they play a sport.

If we do all of these things to develop children into well-rounded people who have academic, athletic, and cultural talents and skills, then it's all the better. If it's so we can relive our glory years through them and get their college paid for, then it's a load of crap. Keep it simple.

It should be more important to teach our children to love and cherish their families than to play piano. It should be more important to teach our children that God gave us our families and called us to help and support one another in every bodily need than to swing a bat or racket. If these principles are at the front of the priority list, then sign the children up for swimming and soccer. If time together as a family—experiencing all the blood, sweat, and tears of what it takes to be a family—is an afterthought, then keep them home to teach them to learn about what life together means. Teach them about their vocation as a son or daughter in a family. Teach them about your vocation and eventually theirs—of being a husband or wife, a mother or father—before you teach them sports, music, or whatever else. And for God's sake, eat freaking dinner together occasionally and talk to each other! If you did that five times a week, you'd be even.

HOME
SWEET HOME

SCOTT KEITH

I find myself thinking about the state of the home more. I'm not referencing the ongoing maintenance tasks that seem ever present when owning a home. I'm not referring to the endless list of chores that every home and every person in the home must contend with to some degree or another. Rather, I am contemplating the actual state of the home in our modern world. Why is home so sweet, as the old saying claims?

In all my ruminations, what I have realized is that the home is the primary place where one engages, interacts, and shares life with his family. Thus a home is a kingdom to every man in that for every good man, husband, and father, the home is a psychological, physical, ethical, intellectual, and certainly spiritual habitat wherein he is unrestricted and free. It is in this freedom that one finds he can truly sacrifice and truly give of himself for the sake of the other, which is his family. The home is unique in that it is the one place where one can give of himself without the risk of diminishing himself. In fact, in the home, to sacrifice is not to make weak, but it is in sacrifice that we prove the old evangelical promise true. Our small, seemingly inconsequential earthly sacrifices—given in the home from a perspective of freedom—point in the most minute of ways to that primary sacrifice that was also won for us, not by coercion or derision, but from freedom for freedom.

Following Chesterton, I think that the home is the only place where a man can truly be free. The home and the family, much like our lives in Christ, are not only paradoxes. The home also solves the paradox that it is. It is where suffering indicates contentment. The home is that place where commanding is obeying. In the home, being the head means being a servant. The family defines the home. The family solves the paradox of what it means to be a man and woman.

> Then the Lord God made a woman from the rib he had taken out of the man, and he brought her to the man. The man said: "this is now bone of my bones and flesh of my flesh; she shall be called woman, for she was taken out of man." That is why a man leaves his father and mother and is united to his wife, and they become one flesh. Adam and his wife were both naked, and they felt no shame. (Gen. 2:22–25)

The home gives us, males and females, a place to live out the calling to leave our fathers and mothers, to be naked and unashamed, and to become fathers and mothers to our own families. In the home, this does not occur from coercion but in vocational freedom.

God the Father is not a passive father. He is the one who has laid the foundation for all families and thus all homes. "For this reason I kneel before the Father, from whom every family in heaven and on earth derives its name" (Eph. 3:14–15). God names a good home, wherein a father and mother act freely to make and keep a family. He names them with His own name. He calls that family and that home to be a shadow of what he is: warm, caring, forgiving, and mostly free.

The modern attack on the family is an attack on Christianity in that it is an attack on God's nature, His character, and His name. By accepting all the attacks from our culture on mother, father, house, home, and family, we watch what God has given us freely drift away. These are the great gifts that He has freely given that we should walk in. These rewards are those with which He blesses us during this season of glad tidings. Good families and good homes serve as pale reflections of God in His goodness.

With our heads held high in the freedom of Christ, let us remember that we are free to be what He has declared we are. We are saved. We are His children. We are redeemed. We are free. We are a part of His family. Let us not forget home and family, and let us see home as that place wherein some of the paradoxes of this life are at the same time revealed and solved. And in remembering, may the home be for you that place where you are free—the place that reminds you that your God is a God of love, warmth, and care—because of the freedom won for you in Christ. God's goodness to us by means of the home is what makes it such a sweet home.

THE HEAD OF THE HOUSE

SCOTT KEITH

American hierarchical sensibilities have been comman-
deered by what I will call the Teamwork Movement. The
Teamwork Movement is exceptionally egalitarian in its
approach to everything, including home life. Thus to even pos-
tulate that there is a "head of the house" must seem to some to
be at once both a dictatorial and oddly transcendent proposition. This proposition may appear dictatorial in nature because
to have a head, a boss, or a leader who is set apart is an offensive
anachronism to the modern reader. In turn, it appears transcendent because I believe we all know that a family needs a head
as much as any person needs a head. The family is the oldest
institution; our idea of family precedes everything including our
modern notions of teamwork and egalitarianism.

So who is the head of your house? Some might say the man
is the head. Others might say it is the woman or the wife in the
home. (In researching this piece, I read a blog wherein a woman
acknowledged that she loved the fact that her husband was the
head of their home, but she admitted she would never say that to
her friends.) And still others would, as I have mentioned, insist
that there is no head. Rather, life in the home is a "headless"

team effort. In my research on fatherhood, one thing has become increasingly clear to me: when we lose the idea of the man as the head of the house, we also lose the idea of what it means to be a good husband and father. Why is this the case? Because once a man's freedom and authority in his own home are taken away, his desire to serve that home in love departs at the same time. It is the freedom provided in the home that allows a man to serve lovingly as provider, protector, sustainer, lover, friend, and forgiver. Once his "headship" is removed, by either usurpation or dispersal, his lack of freedom will inevitably lead to a lack of desire.

I once had a friend that would pick me up every Friday morning at 6:00 a.m. and take me to the men's weekly Bible study sponsored by our little church in Carson City. We would always talk about church stuff while we drove to the restaurant. One morning, we were discussing why the Lutheran Church–Missouri Synod doesn't ordain women, and we were entertaining the idea that they might want to consider it a viable option. At which point, my friend broke in and proclaimed that he did not believe that men should give up their "men-only" prospective roles as pastors and elders in the church. When I asked why, his answer cut me to the quick. He said bluntly, "Men are inspired by freedom yet lazy at heart. If you tell a man he is free to stop being a pastor or elder, he will stop and happily let the women take over. Yet if you tell him he alone is free to serve in these capacities, he will do it with all his heart." I believe the same is true in the home.

Chesterton claims that the definitive aspect of being the "head" of something is that the head is the thing that talks. Speaking, or being the one who talks, is risky business. Words have power. Words change things. Words move people in ways that we cannot even understand. Thus if headship is the power of speech, I think that we ought to bring back the idea of the man as the head of the house. In the home, the father needs authority for one primary reason: he needs the authority to speak the words of forgiveness. Just as pastors need the authority given from Christ to forgive, fathers—for the same purpose—need to feel this authoritative freedom in the home.

In my mind, this does not lessen the role of women or wives in the home. On the contrary, it only strengthens it. Again, paraphrasing Chesterton, the father is the head of the home, while the mother is its heart. In this way, I believe that the structure of a healthy family is such that the mother's authority is differentiated from the father's not so much by its appearance but by how the mother relates to and complements the father's authority. The structure of the mother's authority is defined by how she relates to the father's authority; she affirms her own authority in affirming his. In other words, she is the heart of the forgiveness in the home while he is its mouthpiece. This seemingly dichotomous idea provides an energetic intensity of value to our own ideas of headship.

At the risk of parroting my friend, I think I would say that men are inspired by freedom yet lazy at heart. If you tell a man that he is free to stop being the head of the house and thereby a good, free, authoritative husband and father, he will stop and happily let the women take over these roles. If you tell him he alone is free to serve in these capacities, he will freely do it with all his heart. Men want the authority that allows them to freely love and forgive and not have to lord that authority over their families. Rather, we want to be the talking head of forgiveness that is the mouthpiece of a woman's heart. But we are lazy at heart. If you take the headship from us, we will happily sit on the couch and watch TV instead.

NO FATHER →
NO FAITH?

SCOTT KEITH

A study published by the Pew Research Center entitled "America's Changing Religious Landscape" found that the number of people who self-identify as Christians in the US population is on the decline. At the same time, the number of people in the US who simply do not associate with any type of organized religion is rising. The Pew Research Center claims, "Moreover, these changes are taking place across the religious landscape, affecting all regions of the country and many demographic groups. While the drop in Christian affiliation is particularly pronounced among young adults, it is occurring among Americans of all ages. The same trends are seen among whites, blacks and Latinos; among both college graduates and adults with only a high school education; and among women as well as men."

What are we to make of this? Why is this happening? I'm sure that there are many and varied reasons for this almost clichéd statistical data. Some may even rebuff the data as inconclusive or simply false. Yet when I read the numbers, I was reminded of a few other studies that I ran across while working on my forthcoming book on fatherhood.

Per US Census Bureau data, 43 percent of all children in the United States live in a home in which there is no father. The social ramifications of this sad reality are staggering. Also, per the US Department of Health, 63 percent of all youth suicides occur in fatherless homes. The same agency reports that 90 percent of all runaway children live in a home where there is no father. Further, the Centers for Disease Control and Prevention reported in 2012 that 85 percent of children who show behavior disorders come from fatherless homes—twenty times the national average. A staggering 80 percent of convicted rapists come from fatherless homes (Knight and Prentky, "Developmental Antecedents"). And lastly, a 2014 National Principals Association Report on the state of US schools indicated that 71 percent of all high school dropouts live in fatherless homes.

This crisis even extends into the life of faith and the health and wellness of the church. In 1994, the Swiss carried out a landmark study that revealed the truth about faith in the lives of children. The study found that above all it is the religious practice of the father of the family that determines the future attendance of or absence from church by the children (Low, *Men and Church*). Not surprisingly, the study revealed that if both parents attend church regularly, 33 percent of their adult children would also attend regularly. Also unsurprising is that if only one parent—the mother—attends regularly (and the father is a no-show), a mere 2 percent of adult children will attend regularly. The unexpected result was that if the father alone attends (the mother is the no-show), fully 44 percent of adult children become regular attendees.

In short, if a father is not a believer, the children will most likely not be believers as adults, no matter the faith practices of the mother. If a father is a believer and practices his faith regularly, regardless of the practice of the mother, between 60 and 75 percent of their children will be Christians who regularly attend church. Even a father's irregular faith input and practice will result in more than half of his offspring coming to, staying in, and practicing the faith as adults. In short, fathers matter more than we think when it comes to the faith of their children. In fact, perhaps nothing in a child's faith development matters more than the picture of faith that they see in their own father.

In *Being Dad: Father as a Picture of God's Grace*, I discuss these issues in detail. The parable of the prodigal son serves as the backdrop for the book. This is a powerful story because it provides a picture of the word of forgiveness spoken into a world rightly expecting law. Just when we think condemnation is what is needed, the father steps in and hands out only forgiveness. This is the picture of the Father that Christ paints, and this is the shadow of "fatherness" for which the book will advocate. If fathers are to make a substantive and powerful impact in the lives of their children, it will be by being who God has said they are: little Christ's and forgiveness to their own children.

I hope that *Being Dad: Father as a Picture of God's Grace* has given a gift of a picture of a good father to the readers. In the end, connections will be made between good earthly fathers and the picture of God as our true Father. This book will never be a how-to manual; many specifics will be left out. I am approaching this work through the narrow lens of how good dads who forgive point to the truth of a good God who forgives. There will be no ten steps to better disciplined children here.

As I have said many times, I believe that the law is natural to us, and we need very few tips regarding its implementation in the home. If we choose to be permissive, that is not the law but our own sin. If we choose to be rigidly legalistic in our approach to fatherhood, that is allowing the character of the law to rule over our household in place of the gospel. But if we forgive sins, we cast a reflection that points to a God who forgives in Christ. It is in this way that we understand that fatherhood truly must be at the core of the universe. Again, please remember, perhaps nothing in a child's faith development matters more than the picture of faith that they see in their own father.

NOBODY IS HAPPY WHEN A HELICOPTER IS HOVERING OVER HIS HEAD!

SCOTT KEITH

'll admit it. This is sort of a hobbyhorse for me. I am more and more convinced that parents, specifically helicopter and snow-plow parents, are absolutely destroying an entire generation of people. I would also like to head off at the pass all of you who will say, "There's nothing new under the sun," and "It's always been bad."

Helicopter parents are sending their children into a downward spiral of bleak despair, and it's getting worse. A helicopter parent is a parent who pays extremely close attention to their children's experiences and problems, particularly their educational pursuits. Helicopter parents are so named because they hover over their children's heads like helicopters. Move-in day at the residence halls always brings a gusty storm of buffeting winds as a result of parents' intense fixation on supplying the perfect experience for their children. In other words, they simply won't leave any of us alone. Now, if I feel this way having only interacted with their fixation occasionally, I can only imagine how overwhelmed their children feel. I am not happy when they micromanage my every thought, move, and decision, and I would bet their children are even less happy than I am.

So what does the data say? Those of us who worked in higher education in 2013 knew something was amiss when it seemed that the instances of mental health crises jumped dramatically, but I'm not sure even we knew how bad it was. That same year, a national survey of college counseling center directors was implemented. A stunning 95 percent said the number of students with significant psychological problems is a constant concern on college campuses. Another 70 percent said that the number of students on their campus with severe psychological problems has increased in the past year. They also reported that 24.5 percent of their student clients were taking psychotropic drugs. That is nearly one third of all college students (Gallagher, "National Survey")!

In that same year, the American College Health Association conducted a survey of more than a hundred thousand college students attending 153 different institutions. The survey questioned them regarding their mental health over the last twelve months. (If you want to be depressed, read the entire survey to discover fun facts regarding drug and alcohol use and abuse, as well as sexual activities among college students.) This is what they said:

- Felt things were hopeless = 46.5 percent
- Felt overwhelmed by all you had to do = 84.3 percent
- Felt exhausted (not from physical activity) = 79.1 percent
- Felt very lonely = 57 percent
- Felt very sad = 60.5 percent
- Felt so depressed that it was difficult to function = 31.8 percent
- Felt overwhelming anxiety = 51.3 percent
- Felt overwhelming anger = 38.3 percent
- Attempted suicide = 1.6 percent
- Intentionally cut, burned, bruised, or otherwise injured yourself = 6.5 percent

This movement is apparently not an isolated phenomenon. The 153 schools surveyed were across all fifty states and included both small liberal arts institutions and large R1 research universities. And for those of you who think this is a secular problem, no luck. The survey included religious (Christian) institutions as well as secular schools.

Why are these young adults in a bad state? I have postulated in the past that it may be due in part to the deleterious influence of their parents' high demands and constant badgering. Now, it seems that the "kids" (young adults) are saying it themselves.

In 2012, the *Journal of Adolescence* surveyed nearly five hundred young adults. The survey found that "Initial evidence for this form of intrusive parenting is being linked to problematic development in emerging adulthood . . . by limiting opportunities for emerging adults to practice and develop important skills needed for becoming self-reliant adults" (Padilla-Walker and Nelson, "Black Hawk Down?").

Let me put this into plain language: all children need to learn independently. They need to try to succeed, but they also learn when they try and fail. In fact, this is primarily how they develop coping mechanisms and resiliency. Our fear of failure as parents, which is superimposed on or transferred to our children, often means that parents do whatever is needed to make sure their children never fail. Parents then push their children, their children's teachers, school administrators, school boards, and institutional leadership to ensure that their lovely little Johnny or Susie succeeds and never faces the sting of failure or harm. But the truth is that no matter how annoying and protective parents are, at some time or another their children will fail, they will get hurt, and they will do something wrong—God forbid.

The truth is that they are poor, miserable sinners, just like the rest of us, living in a world that is also plagued by sin. No amount of misguided, overbearing protectiveness will prevent them from sinning, failing, and having the world around them occasionally fall in on them. If parents fail to teach their children this reality, they will be left to figure it out on their own when they are all alone at college. They will feel lied to and betrayed by the people that are supposed to love them the most. They may even feel that without the constant help of the helicopter or the snowplow, they will never be able to accomplish anything, not even a C on a Western Civilizations I exam. Try to imagine the despair that might result if you were successful all your life and then, once on your own for the first time, you feel like you fail at everything you try. The realization that it was never you succeeding but actually your parents succeeding through you might be overwhelming. You may even feel that things are hopeless, that you are overwhelmed by all you have to do, and that you are so exhausted, lonely, sad, and depressed that it is difficult to function, you are overwhelmingly anxious, or you are overwhelmingly angry. You may even try to harm yourself.

Children need to learn a sense of freedom early. When they fail, forgive them, pick them up, dust them off, and set them on the right path again. Try to be a resource and not a burden. Try to help them shovel the obstacles from their path, but don't plow those obstacles out of the way. Rather, if you can, buy them the shovel when it is appropriate and tell them you are proud of them when they've attempted to remove the obstacles themselves. I don't think love means preparing children for a life of misguided achievement and dependence. Rather, love means preparing children to be free to succeed and fail. Love is shown more in forgiveness, mercy, and grace than in misguided hovering. But who knows, I could be wrong; maybe you should ask your children.

THE LAND OF SAFE AND THE HOME OF THE ALWAYS SUCCESSFUL

SCOTT KEITH

While *lunting* with my good friend Josh, we discussed some of the blogs I've posted. He is not a parent yet, though he is very much looking forward to starting a family soon. He asked me my opinion about why modern parents are so insistent on doing things for their children, even when they're grown. As I pondered my answer to his question, he concluded that he thought that maybe it is because modern parents are so fixated on their children being *great*. To which he added, "I want my children to be great too, but . . ."

Before he could finish his ill-fated sentence, I broke in and said that I think the push for constant success under any circumstance is precisely the problem. I added that I have always wanted my children to be free, and if they achieve some measure of success—and I think that they will—I hope it's from a point of freedom, not by means of the compulsion to be great. I also said that I think we have gone from striving to be the land of the free and the home of the brave to the land of the safe and the home of the always successful.

Freedom promotes risk, which makes it very scary. Once set free, children will do what they will do. Freedom produces no guarantee; it only makes promises. Freedom promises that it has more power to motivate than does compulsion. The antithesis is an approach to parenting that focuses only on safety and success. But the success produced is often false because it is a success won without risk. Safety never makes promises and always guarantees. It can make guarantees because it never allows for people to be free.

Ideally, parenting is driven by love at its core. Therefore, we fear our children's failures and attempt to keep them safe by *making* them successful. But all love involves the possibility of rejection. This is what makes love risky business. Risk is not coercive and neither is love. Safety is coercive; it forces our actions into little boxes that can be controlled. If risk is coerced, it is no longer risk but conscripted service. If love is coerced, it ceases to be love and becomes merely a set of programmed responses.

So where am I going with this? In my muddled mind, I see connections—which I'm sure are very imperfect and tenuous connections—between this and an approach to living a life that is of the law or one that is of the gospel.

I have argued that the law always accuses. I still think this is true. But I will concede that in more ancillary ways, the law attempts to restrain, protect, mold, and even guide. But because we are sinners, the law expects failure and thus moves in to attempt to accomplish what it is impotent to do—save. On the other hand, the gospel sets free and expects that its promises will be fulfilled. That is, it promises that sinners will be saved and set free. The gospel also makes good on another one of its promises; it sets the sinner free to produce goodness in return.

I think this is the thrust of Ephesians 2:8-10: "For by grace you have been saved through faith. And this is not your own doing; it is the gift of God, not a result of works, so that no one may boast. For we are his workmanship, created in Christ Jesus for good works, which God prepared beforehand, that we should walk in them." Once freed, that freedom leads to a path where the footsteps God has laid out for the saved sinner are revealed.

The land of the free and the home of the brave is the land where sinners live lives in which they are at the same time saved and sinner. They struggle and fail, and by the grace of God, they occasionally succeed in walking in the path that He has laid out for them. They are brave because God has produced in them a salvation that is so thorough that they know nothing can pluck them out of his hand. "Nor height nor depth, nor anything else in all creation, will be able to separate us from the love of God in Christ Jesus our Lord" (Rom. 8:39). They are safe only in Him, but He risked their loss by setting them free, all the time knowing His grace is sufficient to carry them. Their success is not forced because, if they are successful, it is success that He won for them and granted them in their freedom for the sake of Christ. And He asks them in their freedom to be brave and to persevere as wanderers on the way until He comes to bring them home. Better yet, He forgives them when they corrupt their own freedom, flee to the law, and attempt to keep themselves safe and make themselves successful.

When we raise our kids to be free and brave in Him, we set them free to walk in the path that He has prepared rather than trying to construct the path for them. Freedom promises much, including forgiveness for when that freedom is abused or neglected. Safety guarantees only what it can never accomplish—a life free from pain and fraught with constant success. Our lives in this world are lived as freed saint-sinners until He returns to bring us to the land where true freedom reigns because of Christ.

THE TEN COMMANDMENTS OF THE MODERN PARENT

SCOTT KEITH

I've begun listening to parents as they try to instruct their children. The methods they use are odd to me. It's as if I am watching a Bizarro World where things work backward—a world where up is down and down is up. My question is simple: Is the modern child incapable of learning right from wrong unless concepts are posed as questions?

For instance, if a child needs to learn to eat their broccoli because it is good for them, instead of telling the child, "Eat your broccoli. It is good for you," the modern parent asks the child, "Don't you think that you should eat your broccoli? It's good for you. Isn't it?" The assumption seems to be that if the child figures out the answer on their own, they will be more likely to do the good—eat broccoli—and not the bad—refrain from eating broccoli. Simply because they have been posed the question of the goodness or badness of broccoli, they now have a vested interest in the outcome.

Silly me! I raised my children with imperatives such as "Eat your broccoli! It's good for you" and indicatives like "We're Keiths, and we always eat our broccoli because it's good for us." It never occurred to me to ask them if the Keiths are the sort of people that eat broccoli. Why? They were little children, and little children don't know shit.

This odd state of affairs made me wonder what would have been different if God treated His children as modern parents treat their children. The Ten Commandments might have looked like this:

- Don't think it would be good if you only trusted Me as your God?
- Do you think it is nice to make fun of the name of God?
- You don't want to miss keeping My holy day, do you?
- Don't you think you should be nice to Mommy and Daddy?
- Is killing people a kind way to use your hands?
- Do you think your spouse would have nice feelings if you stick your thing in someone else's thing?
- Is taking what isn't yours nice?
- Do you think your friend would have joyful feelings if she heard you say those things about her?
- Where would your neighbor live if you took his house?
- What would your neighbor have to play with if you took all his things? Don't you think that would make him sad?

Come on, people. Let's get a grip. It's OK, perhaps even appropriate, to tell your children what is right and wrong. It's OK to tell them no. It's OK to tell them to stop it. It's OK to tell them that their behavior is bad and that they are sinners. How else will they learn to forgive and learn that they need forgiveness? Our endless pantomime of inane questions will never produce this.

We need to tell them—not ask "if"—when they are doing something wrong so that they will learn and so that we, their parents, can then proclaim forgiveness. This truth is why the Ten

Commandments are set not as questions to us but rather as commands for us. We are to do these things that we do not do. Thus we know that we need Christ, who has done them in our stead.

Jim Nestingen explains this when he speaks of absolution. He says, "There is a formal way of speaking the Gospel in which the church has historically expressed its confidence: absolution. In the direct and personal declaration of the forgiveness of sin in Christ, the Gospel overlaps the Law, both confirming its accusation and bringing the Law to its end. Only sinners are forgiven; if you are forgiven, you must be one. Yet it is the very act of the absolution, with the freedom it brings, that allows the conclusion of repentance, 'I am a sinner,' to be drawn. Precisely where freedom draws" (Nestingen, "Speech").

If I am a forgiven, then I am a sinner. But I would have never learned that I am a sinner in need of forgiveness if I determined my own state. If God asked me, "Don't you think you are a sinner?" my answer would be a resounding "No!" Therefore, He does not ask me. He tells me through His law. Once I have heard the law condemn me, I then hear the voice of the gospel tell me that I am forgiven in Christ. The voice of the gospel in my absolution frees me before God and frees me to care about and serve my neighbor. And then, having learned both His law and His gospel, I know good and bad, right and wrong, from the position of a person who is free in Christ. I am now free to serve God through serving my neighbor with good.

This cycle of law and gospel, condemnation and absolution, is the point of the Ten Commandments and the point of all good parental instruction—law and gospel, condemnation and absolution, lead to freedom for the good, not inane questions to children.

FATHER ABSENCE AND A SIBLING SOCIETY

SCOTT KEITH

The implications of the data are difficult to escape. One of the world's most prominent fatherhood advocacy organizations is the National Fatherhood Initiative, which was established in 1994, the year I first found out I was going to be a father. On their website, they mention that "per the U.S. Census Bureau, 24 million children in America, one out of three children in America now live in biological father-absent homes. Furthermore, per the national surveys conducted by National Fatherhood Initiative, 9 in 10 parents believe there is a father absence crisis in America" (Sanders, "Father Absence Crisis").

I think that my new friend does not dispute this data as much as he disputes its touting. He wishes for all of us who are concerned about the state of fatherhood in America to resoundingly communicate the important work that dads are doing everywhere rather than the negative impact produced by those who decide not to live their gifts of vocation as fathers. I think I agree.

As a matter of sheer coincidence, as I was in conversation with my new friend, I was also finishing Robert Bly's follow-up to *Iron*

John, entitled *The Sibling Society*. I'm not sure that I would even recommend the book, though I have thoroughly enjoyed it. It is full of some of the same rich wisdom that I found so appealing in *Iron John*, but it lacks the positive character of that work. In other words, I think Bly became depressed while finishing *The Sibling Society*. In fact, Bly as much as admits this toward the end of the work:

> *I began this book in a rather lighthearted tone. I enjoyed the delicious contradictions we see all around us . . . But as I began to realize the extent and implications of the sibling society, my lightheartedness went away, and some weight, as of economics, settled in. The fading of the father as provider in American culture seemed significant to me, and I always assumed that anger against the patriarchal family, some of it justified, was the primary cause. But work on this book has convinced me that other forces have taken part. Those devoted to the bottom line have effectively interposed themselves between father and the family. Part of the effort has been to get at children more easily. The more the parent's dignity and strength are damaged, the more children are open to persuasion. (Bly, Sibling Society, 229–230)*

To clarify, what Bly calls "The Sibling Society" is our current cultural milieu in which we tolerate no one above us and have little regard for those below us. We live as perpetual adolescents, taking selfies and looking around to see if anyone has noticed us. Rather than looking anywhere for direction—to father, mother, or God—we tend to ask one simple question: "Am I famous yet?" Our culture, Bly says (in the 1990s), has brought down all forms of hierarchy because at times hierarchy—which is based solely on power—led to abuse. In the process, we have lost the desire and ability to look up or down. Bly is correct; these cold realities are very depressing.

It was for these very reasons that I was wary of placing any of the negative statistics regarding fatherhood in my book *Being Dad: Father as a Picture of God's Grace*. I was concerned that I might use only those statistics that benefited my argument and neglect those that suggested conclusions that did not line up with my way of thinking. This confusion is what happens when we focus on statistics. The data the "stats" give us are tools to an end, not the end unto themselves. Thus I attempted to paint a positive picture of what God accomplishes through the gift of fathers rather than simply communicating sometimes depressing statistics. Accordingly, the statistics were reduced to three paragraphs on pages three and four.

Those of us who are concerned about the state of our culture need to look beyond the sociological data and tired pop psychology and see our situation afresh. The truth is that fathers have a great calling and opportunity. God has given us the most wonderful gift we will ever receive on this side of glory, which is the gift of our children. Accordingly, he has called us to be fathers, and this is our primary vocation.

We may do many other things. We may hold many other vocations. But if we have children, we are first and foremost parents and, in my case, a father. The impact that one good father, given as a gift from God to His children, has on the life of his children is immeasurable. He can lead them to the one true faith through the words of forgiveness, the gospel itself, flowing from his mouth. He can teach his children to look up to a God who is good and gracious and to look down to those people that God has placed in their lives for them to serve freely.

If we live in a sibling society, as Bly suggests and I think we do, the only cure is to live our vocations as parents to the best of our ability, asking for God's grace and forgiveness when we fail. The data, even excellent data, only have the potential to show us half of the picture. The other half of the picture is more than just the other half, after all; it is all in all. God, who is gracious to us because of Christ, is our Father. He has set us in this world to do His will and fulfill our vocations as children, siblings, mothers, and fathers. Because of that same Christ, he will forgive us when we fail.

Those of us who are in Christ have always known that we live in a sibling society. We have brothers and sisters in Christ all over the world who look up to a God who is good to us for the sake of Christ and down to others, our neighbors, whom we are now free to serve for the sake of Christ.

HAPPY WIFE, HAPPY LIFE

SCOTT KEITH

Disclaimer: Before I write this blog and describe how awful I believe the concept of "happy wife, happy life" is, please allow me to provide a few disclaimers. First, I love my wife. We have been married for twenty-one years and have raised three beautiful children together. I can honestly say that she is the love of my life. Second, like all couples, we have had good times and bad. We have treated one another extremely well, and at times we have both treated one another poorly and shamefully. We are somewhat typical as far as that goes. We do not have a perfect marriage—nothing is perfect this side of glory—but we do have a good marriage. She is for me, and I am for her.

THE ARGUMENT

As far as I understand the mantra, the argument goes something like this: If a husband does whatever is necessary and lives as though all that matters in life is his wife's happiness, then he too will be happy. Presumably, a husband will also be happy because his wife will know that come what may, she is right and he is wrong, and he will capitulate to her better judgment. The argument was best summed up by a meme I recently saw entitled, "The Golden Rule for a Happy Marriage." It went like this:

Rule #1: The wife is always right.
Rule #2: When you feel that she is wrong, slap yourself and refer to rule #1.

YOU CAN'T MAKE ANOTHER PERSON HAPPY

I have several problems with this inane modern banter. First and foremost is the reality that no one person can make another person consistently happy, no matter what he or she does. Either people are happy in their situations or they are not. Allow me to clarify. I believe that being a husband or a wife is a vocation given by God. God is He who calls us into relationships with one another for a myriad of reasons, including procreation. But I cannot make my wife happy within our relationship no matter what I do unless she is already somewhat accepting of her vocation as wife and generally content with her life. If I am content in our marriage, she is generally more content as well and vice versa. But what kind of person would she be if what made her happy was that I was made miserable by serving her every whim? Do we not call these types of people "evil despots"? If the husband's happiness doesn't matter at all, and the wife's happiness alone is the goal, what incentive does any man have to get married? Perhaps we all shouldn't wonder so much why young men overall no longer care about marriage when we go around saying foolish crap like "happy wife, happy life."

SOCIAL JUSTICE WARRIORS

Second, I think that this phrase is an outgrowth of the overall social justice war that has been going on since the sixties and is now embodied by the modern social justice warrior. A social justice warrior is a blogger, activist, or commentator who is prone to engage in lengthy and hostile debates against others on a range of issues concerning social injustice, identity politics, marriage equality, gender, and political correctness. These people have been engaging in a social blitzkrieg over the last decade, and they seem to have won. The systematic goal of the social justice warrior is to tear down any remnant of the old white male patriarchal system and replace it with one that is more inclusive. The phrase "happy wife, happy life" affirms the social justice idea that men have been happy and in control long enough, and now it is women's time to rule. This usurpation of time-honored norms might be all well and good if, in the process, men—husbands and fathers specifically and Christian marriages even more precisely—hadn't been completely trampled underfoot.

IT IS NOT ALL ABOUT HAPPINESS

Third, though it is wonderful when two people are happy in a marriage—or just the wife per the mantra—marriage is not all about happiness. The sheer reality of the sinful world in which we live is that some of us are never happy and most of us, though we may feel content and blessed, are not consistently happy. Although marriage is not all about happiness, God has given us to one another to help one another and be blessed by one another. But I digress. "It is not good for man to be alone," God said. "Let us create for him a helpmate" (Gen. 2:18). Husband and wife are to help one another and make it through together. Wives are made for their husbands. Husbands are called to love and cherish their wives. Happiness is nice, but God's call that, "Man shall leave his father and his mother and hold fast to his wife" is good. When this "holding fast" results in mutual and not one-sided happiness, it is even better, perhaps even great.

CHRIST IN THE MIDDLE

Fourth, the apostle Paul turns this phrase on its head:

> Submit to one another out of reverence for Christ. Wives, submit your-
> selves to your own husbands as you do to the Lord. For the husband

is the head of the wife as Christ is the head of the church, his body, of which he is the Savior. Now as the church submits to Christ, so also wives should submit to their husbands in everything. Husbands, love your wives, just as Christ loved the church and gave himself up for her to make her holy, cleansing her by the washing with water through the word, and to present her to himself as a radiant church, without stain or wrinkle or any other blemish, but holy and blameless. In this same way, husbands ought to love their wives as their own bodies. He who loves his wife loves himself. (Eph. 5:21–28)

We are to submit to one another in reverence to Christ. Christ is in the middle of our marital relationship. He established it; He loves it; He sustains it; and He is the one who redeems both husband and wife.

FREE BEFORE GOD, SERVANT TO ALL

Fifth, this is part of what Luther means when he claims in *Christian Liberty*, "A Christian man is the most-free lord of all, and subject to none; a Christian man is the most dutiful servant of all, and subject to everyone." Wives are not served at the expense of their husbands, and husbands are not served at the cost of their wives. Rather, those of us who are in Christ are free before God because of Christ. In Christ, the law no longer has the power to condemn us before God. We are now free to serve one another in love, not because of threats or fear. We serve first those God has called into our lives in the form of family and work our way out from there to our neighbors in the world. What I despise most about the mantra is that it brings a veiled threat into our freedom in Christ. I am free to love and serve my wife because Christ has set me free. I do not love her out of threat that my life will be unhappy if I don't make her happy. Rather, I love and serve her because Christ has set me free and called her into my life so that I might freely love her with all that I have. And though my effort to love her is often too little, God wraps me in His grace and for the sake of Christ forgives me for that as well.

YOU ARE FREE INDEED!

"So if the Son sets you free, you will be free indeed" (John 8:36). So what is left? What is left is to live in Christ. Live in His mercy; live in His grace; live in His freedom; live in His calling to others; live in His love first shown to you, which you know because of Christ. Show His love to those whom He has called to be your neighbor. Live in your marriage every day knowing you wake up next to a child of God who because of Christ is free to serve you, and feel free to serve her and make her happy in return.

WOMEN WEAKEN LEGS!

ROSS ENGEL

One of my favorite movies of all time is *Rocky*. I love the entire series, minus the disappointment that was *Rocky V*. In the first film, Rocky is training hard for his shot at the champ. He lands himself a girlfriend, the lovely and slightly awkward Adrian, who later becomes his wife. When his trainer, Mick, finds out that he's involved with a woman, he grumbles at Rocky and tells him point blank, "Women weaken legs!" At that point, Rocky reluctantly agrees not to fool around with Adrian anymore.

Rocky goes on to fight Apollo Creed, does well, and in the process sets up the *Rocky* franchise for another seven films and counting. He listened to Mick and prevailed!

"Women weaken legs."

In my sports career, I often heard such a saying from coaches. Every coach from junior high through college had their own way of scaring my teammates and me away from women, who all apparently have the skill to "weaken legs." For those wanting to perform their best at a sport, dating was forbidden. Now, I'll readily admit that this wasn't a problem for me for the first seventeen years of my life. My dorky haircut, crooked teeth, and glasses did a fine job at keeping the girls away, so I had an abundance of time to focus on my sports.

When I got to seminary, I recall a now-departed professor who offered similar words of encouragement to the married guys to abstain from the joys of "husband and wife-ing" on Saturday nights so that we would be "better focused on the preaching task" on Sunday morning. His words were a bit more vivid and slightly more disturbing than I think the Jagged Mafia is ready for. But apparently, even in the preaching task, "women weaken legs."

I do understand the rationale behind such encouragement. It is echoed by Paul in 1 Corinthians 7 when he writes, "Stop depriving one another, except by agreement for a time, so that you may devote yourselves to prayer, and come together again so that Satan will not tempt you because of your lack of self-control. But this I say by way of concession, not of command." Paul encourages husbands and wives to abstain from the act of one-fleshing for a specific purpose, and it seems to me that the purpose is so that they would not be distracted from the things of our Lord—prayer and those precious means of grace that our Lord uses to strengthen us in our faith.

Notice that the text continues with encouragement for husbands and wives to reconnect after a time of abstaining for the purpose of being stronger together in the face of temptation. I think there is more to the returning to be together than just a combined strength in the face of temptation. I truly believe that husbands and wives do better in their vocations of husband and wife—and in every other arena of life—when they find their strength and joy in each other and their one-flesh union.

There have been many studies done on the positive and negative physiological and psychological effects of one-fleshing, but this isn't a health sciences thesis. I'm more interested in the God-given stations and vocations that we have in life and how, when husbands and wives participate in the marital union that God has blessed them with, they find greater enjoyment in life, strength for the day, and function more effectively in every area of their lives than when the physical aspect of their marriages is missing.

When I perform a wedding, part of the wedding address includes these words: "The union of husband and wife in heart, body, and mind is intended by God for the mutual companionship, help, and support that each person ought to receive from the other, both in prosperity and adversity. Marriage was also ordained so that man and woman may find delight in one another" (*Lutheran Service Book*, 275). When husbands and wives find delight in one another, they aren't as likely to be living in fear or wonder about the status of their relationship. They are more likely to feel secure and so then are also freed up to do whatever tasks God has given them to do, both in the home and in the workplace.

Sometimes couples find themselves stuck in a habit of separation. Sure, they're going through the day-to-day tasks of living under the same roof and even sleeping in the same bed, but the joy is missing. The intimacy and joy of delighting in one another isn't there, so their life together suffers. Tempers flare. Trust or faithfulness can be questioned. The desire to help and serve each other dwindles. Even the tasks in one's career can suffer when husbands and wives forget to take delight in one another.

So toss away the temptations to marginalize your marriage. Stop going through the motions as husband and wife. Don't let the intimate bond that you have as husband and wife fall by the wayside. Don't let the harried pace of life weaken the bond that God united you in when you said, "I do!" Go on a date. Plan a night to be together. Send flowers. Leave messages of love and intimacy. Talk. Make your spouse and the union you have with them a priority. Turn off the television. Put down the stupid phone. Stop endlessly scrolling through Facebook. Get rid of all those distractions that have no point beyond their own continuance. They only get in the way of you being a husband to your wife or a wife to your husband. It's simple, though not easy, but I guarantee that it is absolutely worth it.

St. Paul's encouragement to the Corinthians was to deprive one another of the act of one-fleshing for only a short time but then to come back together so that both man and woman, husband and wife, would be strengthened and encouraged in their life together.

Taking delight in our spouses does not weaken our legs or anything else in our lives. Husbands, love your wives and be willing to give your life for them. Wives, love your husbands. And husbands and wives, get to it! Take delight in one another! Find joy in all the tasks, great and small, that our Lord has given you to do.

I CAN DOOEY IT!

SCOTT KEITH

Our youngest child, Autumn, has always been very competent. She learned how to do things very early; walking, talking, and tying her shoes all came quickly and were seemingly natural to her. When we would teach her to do something, as soon as she had even the slightest idea of how to do it, she would push our hands away and say, "I can dooey it." "I can dooey it" has been her motto from that time forward.

When she was twelve, she started babysitting two days a week for some friends of the family. At the start, the family had four children, one of whom has special needs. Soon after, they had their fifth child, and Autumn was there twice a week every week doing her best to be of some help to this very busy family. Last year, she added to her list of duties by taking on the task of watching the infant of another friend once a week. So, three days a week—about fifteen hours a week in total—she worked for these families, watching their children, teaching them, helping to potty train them, dressing them, and filling in wherever necessary. This was all in addition to her standard homeschool curriculum while taking two college courses a semester.

My point is not to brag about Autumn—though I am always ready to do that. Rather, my point is to examine the reaction of other people. Almost without fail, when we tell people about her babysitting endeavors, they inevitably say something like, "Sheesh, you'd better be careful letting her do all that. She's never going to want to be a mother." Comments such as these always confuse me. Their argument seems to be that giving teenagers responsibility will cause them never to want responsibility again.

To be honest with you, I think this line of thinking is dangerous. In fact, I know it is. It is another manifestation of the helicopter and snowplow parent mind-sets. These parents seek to remove all responsibility and burden from the lives of children, and they instead produce anguish and anxiety in those same children. Removing legitimate vocational pursuits from the lives of our children and teenagers will only cause them to disregard the idea of vocation altogether. It is in living our Christian vocations that we learn how beautiful the gift of vocation is.

I am not trying to say that every child needs to do as much as Autumn is doing. Rather, this is to say that we ought to stop being afraid that we will repel our children from the idea of vocation by teaching them to live it. If we are truly free to love God and serve our neighbor on account of what Christ has done for us, then we should not fear our freedom to serve one another in vocation.

I think that one of the reasons we fear teenage responsibility is because we have a flawed idea of vocation in general. I think we have begun to see it as the world sees it—as merely a job. Article VI of the *Augsburg Confession* says, "Also they teach that this faith is bound to bring forth good fruits, and that it is necessary to do good works commanded by God, because of God's will, but that we should not rely on those works to merit justification before God." Good works are necessary for the Christian life.

A fundamental misunderstanding of good works prevails in modern Christianity. What the *Augsburg Confession* speaks of here is not necessarily helping old ladies across the street with their groceries or going on a short-term mission trip to Africa. Rather, what I am suggesting is that we need to reconsider what living the life of a Christian through vocation means. Availing oneself of the proclaimed word and rightly administered sacraments and sharing that gospel with those God has placed in our lives is living life as a Christian. Serving one another in love through our various vocations—husband, father, mother, wife, daughter, son, worker, and student—are our Christian vocations.

Dr. Gene Veith explains this concept well in his book *God at Work—Your Christian Vocation in All of Life*: "For the Christian, love of neighbor becomes something consciously felt, as faith becomes active in love. Though we sin against our vocations, as we grow in Christ the everyday task set before us can be motivated and shaped by love."

Martin Luther was once approached by a man who desperately wanted to serve the Lord more fervently. He asked Luther, "What should I do to serve the Lord?" as if to imply that he should become a monk or a priest. Luther asked him, "What is your work now?"

"I'm a cobbler."

Much to the cobbler's surprise, Luther replied, "Then make a good shoe, and sell it at a fair price."

Funny, Luther didn't say, "Well, one thing is for sure. Don't make any more shoes or you'll certainly get sick of it and never want to make a shoe again!" By believing that our children will be burdened by vocational pursuits if allowed to undertake them in their teen years, we spoil them on the idea of Christian vocation in general. Service to our neighbor then becomes self-centered and woeful.

I don't think that babysitting too much will cause my daughter not to want children any more than I believe that reading will cause her not to desire to read in the future. In fact, I think that learning to serve these children in love might teach her the joys—and frustrations—of parenting her own children in love someday. Our service in love to our neighbor is full of joy and frustration. Love through both joy and frustration is our promise and our blessing.

We are saved sinners who are stuck together until that time when the Lord brings us home or when He comes again in glory.

We live here free to be all that He has already declared we are in Christ. We are His children called to be His people. We are called to stand before Him freely and serve one another freely. As Jim Nestingen and Gerhard Forde wrote in *Free to Be*, this is the story of death and birth: "The death of the old you that fights and struggles against God, your neighbors, and the earth; the birth of the new you, born in the waters of Baptism and sustained in God's speaking. This is the new you God is making in you, the you who is a believer. As God makes you new, you will discover the freedom that God gives, the freedom that is given with joy and the certainty of God's promise" (Nestingen, Forde, and Bruning, *Free to Be*). Why would we ever teach our children otherwise?

TO ESTHER

SCOTT KEITH

10 APRIL 2016

Dearest Esther,

I love you. You were born on April 7, 2016, and you were baptized into Christ today. When I first saw you, my heart leaped for joy. I had many of the same feelings looking at you as I did when I first saw your dad, Uncle Josh, and Aunt Autumn when they were born. But seeing you was different. When I saw you, I not only rejoiced for myself and your grandmother, but I also got to celebrate with your dad and your mom as well. You are their child, and by that, I am your grandfather.

Your baptism today was a glorious event. In an odd bit of serendipity, just this week my students at the university asked me why baptism is so important. I used you as an example. I hope you don't mind. I told them that because you were baptized, we—those who love you the most—have complete assurance that upon your baptism, you are God's child. He has claimed you, made you His, and redeemed you from sin, death, and the power of the devil. You, my dearest Esther, are God's child! Though you belong to your mom and dad, your Heavenly Father, for the sake of Christ, has put you in His hand and will never let you go.

Later, as you grow and as your mom and dad catechize you in the Christian faith, you'll learn that the words of scripture are clear. Matthew 28 says, "Go therefore and make disciples of all nations, baptizing them in the name of the Father and of the Son and of the Holy Spirit." The book of Acts tells us in chapter 2, "Repent and be baptized [passive imperative] every one of you in the name of Jesus Christ for the forgiveness of your sins and you will receive the gift of the Holy Spirit. For this promise is for you and for your children and for all who are far off, everyone whom the Lord calls to Himself." The apostle Peter says in 1 Peter chapter 3: "Baptism, which corresponds to this, now saves you, not as a removal of dirt from the body but as an appeal to God for a good conscience, through the resurrection of Jesus Christ." The apostle Paul says in Romans chapter 6, "Do you not know that all of us who have been baptized into Christ Jesus were baptized into his death? We were buried therefore with Him by baptism into death, in order that, just as Christ was raised from the dead by the glory of the Father, we too might walk in newness of life. For if we have been united with Him in a death like his, we shall certainly be united with Him in a resurrection like his." And finally, he also tells us in Titus chapter 3, "But when the goodness and loving kindness of God our Savior appeared, He saved us, not because of works done by us in righteousness, but per His own mercy, by the washing of regeneration and renewal of the Holy Spirit, whom He poured out on us richly through Jesus Christ our Savior, so that being justified by His grace we might become heirs according to the hope of eternal life."

You see, God wanted you to be His child. He used ordinary things like water and words from Pastor Rhode's lips to make you His own. I love you so much, and seeing the life-giving water and the word pour over your head, cleansing you of all your sin, made me cry. Nothing could make me prouder of your mom and dad than watching them bring you to the saving waters of Holy Baptism. For that, and for all other things that He brings about for your benefit, I say, "Thanks be to God!"

I leave you today with the words of a hymn that I once used to comfort a friend of mine who had lost one of his children. The words bring comfort and peace to me, and I hope to your mom and dad also, because they clearly present the truth of what happens when a sinner is brought before God in Holy Baptism. I won't print all the stanzas here, just a few to help you remember what happened that day.

> *"God's own child, I gladly say it: I am baptized into Christ!*
> *He, because I could not pay it, gave my full redemption price.*
> *Do I need earth's treasures many? I have one worth more than any*
> *That brought me salvation free, Lasting to eternity!"*

> *"Satan, hear this proclamation: I am baptized into Christ!*
> *Drop your ugly accusation; I am not so soon enticed.*
> *Now that to the font I've traveled, all your might has come unraveled,*
> *And, against your tyranny, God, my Lord, unites with me!"*

("I Am Baptized into Christ," Lutheran Service Book)

Esther, your life is an amazing gift from God, and an earthly death will not have the last word with you. You are baptized into Christ! Satan can rage and rail against you, but his words are empty threats. None of his accusations will ever have victory over you. You have traveled to the font where sin and death have come unraveled and have been washed away in the waters of life. You, dear Esther, are baptized into Christ.

I love you, my dearest Esther, and I write this so that one day you'll read it and remember the miracle that brought you to life eternal. Your life, in this world and in the next, is a gracious gift from God given to all of us on account of Christ. I thank Him so much that He has given you to your mom and dad, and in a different way to your grandma and me, to love and to cherish. We praise Him for when we succeeded in fulfilling our vocations as parents and grandparents, and we ask for His and your forgiveness for when we fail.

Please know that I am always here for you and that I love you.

Love,
Grandpappy

SCARED SHITLESS

CALEB KEITH

I vividly remember the comments, advice, and criticism of pretty much everybody I encountered when I was preparing to get married. The most common response to this information was "How old are you?" or "I hope you know what you're getting into." Many others asserted that I was throwing my life and freedom away, while only a few responded joyously or with legitimate loving concern. Questions and comments like the examples above were shallow and general concerns about age and autonomy. I was under the same type of scrutiny two years later while I awaited the birth of my daughter.

Instead of questions, most people gave me grim news when they heard that I was about to be a dad. The most common messages were "Say good-bye to sleep" and "Your world is going to be destroyed." These are fair warnings to be sure, but I'd heard them hundreds of times, and what I didn't hear was positive or hopeful news. I received the occasional "I hope you're excited!" but it was usually paired with the other warnings. It seemed as if all I should be excited for was the end of my sanity. I was tired of people telling me how scared I should be, because I was already scared shitless.

With all the negative questioning I received at the time of my marriage and the fearmongering before the coming of my first child, I no longer wonder why young people abhor the adult world. Christians bemoan the degraded cultural milieu and the shallow sexual ethics that plague society. Yet we fill our children's heads with nothing but fear when it comes to getting married or having children. Why would I want a spouse if it is the end of my freedom, and why have a child if it is the end of my world? For every downside of being married young, I can think of five positive or valuable elements. I view fatherhood in the same light. This is thanks to my own father and mother, who, rather than scare me, encouraged my wife and me, exciting us with the good to come from parenthood rather than the terror that might ensue. As I said earlier, I am scared shitless, but I am filled even more with happiness and anticipation. This happiness is rooted in Christ and the new life that is about to enter His fold. Even more exciting than Esther's birth was her new birth in the waters of baptism. In the promise of the word, I get to share in true life with a child whom God has called Erika and me to raise. In the face of fear, I rejoice in the comfort of our Lord and the blessings he brings through children. I encourage every reader to do the same. Let's stop holding marriage and parenthood captive to fear and instead emphasize how God works through such humbling and challenging vocations.

ADULTERY

CALEB KEITH

It seems that there is a new hacking scandal every other week. Credit card numbers, names, and addresses are regularly stolen from retailers and online marketplaces. One that probably affected at least one person you know was the 2013 Target hack, through which over forty million credit card numbers were stolen. Shoppers panicked, banks reacted in a frenzied rush to attempt to protect customers, and Target had a massive PR problem to deal with. How about when thirty-seven million individuals' personal information was stolen from Ashley Madison? Ashley Madison is a dating website with a twist. It is designed and marketed toward married adults looking for affairs. Their motto is "Life is short. Have an affair."

After the Ashley Madison hack, thirty-seven million adulterers sat at home biting their nails, hoping that all the hackers wanted was their credit card information. With one stroke of a keyboard, lives could be turned upside down and families torn apart. Commenters on the Internet were up in arms over who was to blame. Was it Ashley Madison, the hackers, or the adulterers who were at fault for such a mishap? The answer seems pretty clear cut to me: don't cheat on your husband or wife, and you'll never have to worry about getting caught. However, the ethical realities of today's world, or at least the loudest voices on the Internet, believe that the only thing wrong here is the "stealing." For every comment that says, "I guess they shouldn't have cheated," there are ten that say, "The idea that you're OK with the theft because it conforms to your moral code is disturbing to me." The sexual ethics of Western culture are all over the map, making conversation difficult when someone fires back with "Well, that's just your moral code, not mine."

Adultery and sex are big issues, and Ashley Madison hooks up cheaters. Few people seem to be able to keep it in their pants—porn is the number-one search on the Internet. Sexual sins have always been an issue, though; just take a peek at the Old Testament! What surprises me today is not that sex and adultery are problems but how we respond to them. As a young married man, I was the recipient of endless questioning and lecturing from anyone who could grab my ear during the six months leading up to my wedding. Here are some of the things that were said:

> "Why are you getting married? Don't you know you have your whole life ahead of you?"
> "Fine, get married, but just don't have kids until you're done with school."
> "You haven't been dating long enough to know you want to spend your life with her."

The list goes on. The common theme across all of these lines is that success, happiness, love, and sex should remain separate. Don't have sex before you get married, but date somebody for six years, graduate college, and get a job before you even start to talk about tying the knot.

Sex is tied to marriage, and marriage is reserved for after you've already lived life and had as much fun and success as you can achieve. More often than not, the easy answer for my generation is to untie sex from marriage in order to be happy, live life successfully, and still have all the sex you want. When marriage is described as the last major step after everything good in life has already happened, it's easy to see why services like Ashley Madison have thirty-seven million names sitting on a server. As Christians, it's easy to get caught up in the moral conversation about sex, but it only makes us look like moralists standing on a high horse. In a conversation with Dr. Jeff Mallinson, he said to me, "Virtue thinking encourages us to stop asking what our genitals are allowed to touch and start remembering that if we get our hearts in the right place our genitals will follow." The real conversation isn't about sex or adultery; it's about how we talk about and describe love, sex, and marriage.

Talking about marriage as if it were a plague or the last step before death encourages people, young and old alike, to go outside of marriage to fulfill their sexual desires. Marriage is an amazing gift from God that brings joy and fulfillment through shared experiences, forgiveness, hard work, and even sex. We should work together to stop hiding those gifts behind a wall of fear and instead share the joy of marriage with our friends, family, and children.

PARALYZED
BY FEAR

CALEB KEITH

On April 7, 2016, my beautiful daughter Esther Lily Joy Keith was born. My wife and I were blessed with a quick and easy labor and a very healthy daughter. However, what followed the relatively easy birth was an uncomfortable forty-eight hours in the hospital watching my wife and daughter get poked and prodded by nurses and doctors. Every test came back perfect, and after twenty-four of those forty-eight hours, my wife's OBGYN was prepared to discharge her so we could go home to rest as a family. Unfortunately, she was not authorized to discharge my daughter, and the hospital pediatrician wouldn't let us go despite Esther's lack of complications and health issues. When my wife Erika and I finally got home, we could breathe, and my baby girl was finally able to rest without being tested every two hours.

When Erika and I took Esther to her first doctor's appointment, it was essentially two hours of questioning steeped in sheer fear. Most of the concerns were not about direct health problems with my daughter but with the probability or possibility of hundreds of dangers. The questions were absurd: "Will anybody who smokes ever encounter this baby? Do you own a firearm? Will you let anybody hold her who isn't completely up to date on their vaccines?" These three questions only begin to scratch the surface. Five minutes in, I began to question how any babies before this point in time ever survived. Above all, what I realized is that we live in a society paralyzed by fear.

As a new parent, I am already scared enough about the things I might do wrong or neglect to do. The last thing I want is another two-hundred items on my list of worries. I love my daughter, and I want nothing but the best for her, but I am not going to give all my family and friends the fifth degree about their own vaccinations. This is not because I don't care about my daughter's health but because I refuse to live in a constant state of fear. I will not let the first days I spend with my daughter be defined or ruled by fear. How could I when the true fears of sin, death, and the devil have been erased by Christ's death and resurrection? Esther, Erika, and I share in that gift through our baptisms, and through faith we are saved and given new life. The new or sanctified life is not one of fear but is one of hope, joy, and grace. My goal as a father and a Christian in the world is to proclaim Christ for the forgiveness of sins by which all fear loses its true power. I will always care for the health needs of my daughter and family, not out of fear, but in the joyous hope that I will share in a long life with my daughter where our relationship is one empowered and freed by Christ. Thanks be to God for such amazing freedom.

THE FATHER IN THE MIDDLE

SCOTT KEITH

One Father's Day weekend, I was in Cadillac, Michigan at Joel Hess's church teaching on *Being Dad: Father as a Picture of God's Grace*. As I say in the book, the story is the tale of two lost and found sons and a dad who has been in the middle the whole time. This is the tale of the Father who loves us and sent His Son in order that we, through His death and resurrection, might be like one who "was dead, and is alive" and be claimed as His own child.

I am struck by the fact that the parable is essentially the story of two sons trying to make a deal with their father by means of righteous proclamation and pathetic confession. I'm struck because we also try to make deals with our Heavenly Father. But here is the thing: Our deals are not wanted. The dead cannot make deals, nor can they confess. They only need to be brought back to life. It is as Capon notes: "Confession is not a transaction, not a negotiation to secure forgiveness; it is the last gasp of a corpse that finally can afford to admit it's dead and accept resurrection" (Capon, *Kingdom, Grace, Judgment*).

The way the parable unfolds is unexpected. What happens to them makes no sense from any perspective. The gospel is the same way. It makes no sense; it's a stumbling block. It's probably not possible to completely capture the mystery of what it means to be saved by God in Christ in any parable or story. Yet in this tale, we have some inkling of what it might mean. The father is in the house. It is always safe to come home.

The overall theme is that *you* can always come home. Jesus has made you, a dead thing, alive! The calf has been killed, and thus the celebration that is the Father's house *must* begin. His word of forgiveness will always be free to you. We rely on the Father's strong word of grace because when He pronounces us righteous because of Christ, we are made alive. This is the only thing we can rely on. It is fitting to celebrate and be glad, for these brothers and sisters to your left and right were dead and are alive; *you* were dead and are alive. You were lost and now are found! It is fitting to celebrate! The Father's words to us all are the words of life and raise us from that dead state.

God has given us these parables so that we might rely on them and share them and so that we might speak God's words of life, imparting faith, hope, and life. His word on our lips kills and makes alive. Capon gives us one more insight into the purpose of these tales when he says that in this tale we see clearly that the last judgment will be the ultimate vindication: "For the simple reason that everybody will have passed the only test that God has, namely, that they are all dead and risen in Jesus. Nobody will be kicked out for having a rotten life because nobody there will have any life but the life in Jesus. God will say . . . 'You were dead and are alive again; you were lost and are found: put on the funny hat and step inside'" (Capon, *Kingdom, Grace, Judgement*). You can always come home. Put on the funny hat and step into the party. Jesus has made you, a dead thing, alive!

C. S. Lewis says, "The Prodigal Son at least walked home on his own feet. But who can duly adore that love which will open the high gates to a prodigal who is brought in kicking, struggling, resentful, and darting his eyes in every direction for a chance of escape? The hardness of God is kinder than the softness of men, and His compulsion is our liberation" (Lewis, *Surprised by Joy*).

The compulsion of the Father is to set us free from sin, death, and the power of the devil at any cost. And for the sake of Christ, this is exactly what He does. This is the only hope we have, given through the grace of the Father to us prodigals everywhere. You can rely on that.

Now, it is time for you to drop dead. Shut up, forget about your stupid life, go inside, and pour yourself a tall drink.

Remember: "The hardness of God is kinder than the softness of men, and His compulsion is our liberation" (Lewis, *Surprised by Joy*).

And to that, I think we can all say Amen!

IF GOD IS BETTER THAN MY FATHER, HE'S REALLY GOOD

RICK RITCHIE

This writing is the product of self-reflection on my twelfth birthday. I was into dolphins that year, which was 1978. I was a weird kid. I was more into *Close Encounters of the Third Kind* than *Star Wars*. We went to Sea World so I could pet dolphins.

My dad was a good sport. He drove us to San Diego, and I quickly found the dolphin tank. I thought we would spend the whole day petting dolphins. I hadn't considered what my parents would spend their time doing. My dad thought there might be other shows worth seeing. I'm not sure how it would have gone if it hadn't been for some providential intervention, but at some point, as we had been there for some time, a dolphin pointed his blowhole toward my face and exhaled. It was like some combination of a fart and bad breath, the bad breath making the fart barely tolerable. I was now done with the dolphins. It was time for the other shows.

Now, as big as all that was at the time, something else ended up being more prominent that day. It wasn't any of the other shows, most of which were really cheesy, even at the time—pearl divers, seals, and some planted person in the audience who knew how to ride dolphins perfectly after hopping on one foot and "accidentally" falling into the tank. Rather, it was that when it came time to ride a hydrofoil in the harbor, my dad bought a Sea World sweatshirt for me so I wouldn't be cold. This was back when many parents spent very freely in amusement parks. And while some (they're called women) especially need to be given a gift on time like clockwork, I valued most the gift that came outside of an expected ritual. This sweatshirt was not a wrapped gift that had been planned in advance. I wore it more than I should have, as it was abundantly symbolic to me.

When I think of God the Father, I know He must be better than this. Long ago, in third grade (I seemed to have a crisis every three years as a child), I had been thinking that I couldn't continue as a Christian because believing in Christianity did not—at least at the time—seem like believing in other things. I would put off thoughts of this until I was elderly. But Narnia got me thinking that if God was like Aslan, then it would turn out OK. That became a benchmark. C. S. Lewis hadn't invented something better than the real thing.

Likewise, God the Father Almighty is good, and He must be good in ways that surpass my earthly father. When Jesus defers to his Heavenly Father, He already knows what a good father does. He knew this from Joseph. What would it mean to have parents who took you down to Egypt away from all that was familiar to get to safety during a crisis? Whatever else, it meant that Jesus had a benchmark. If His earthly father was this good, then His Heavenly Father must be even better. This point must be fundamental to our consciousness. It is one of the most basic categories any of us has.

Whatever your earthly father did or did not do, his goodness is a benchmark. As a spiritual exercise, I commend to you the following: think of some act where his goodness really surprised you, and then consider that your Heavenly Father is good in this very way, only more so. We all have different earthly fathers. For some, our only concept of our Heavenly Father is that He must be better than our earthly father across the board. This might not be helpful for some; I'm very sorry if that's the case. But for most, even where there was failure and disappointment, there are some incidents that provide benchmarks. Consider what that means for you if it is true. What if God is better than that, not in some mathematical and abstract way, but on that very point? What does it mean?

THROUGH THE FATHER'S EYES

PAUL KOCH

I remember quite fondly an unexpected trip that my dad and I took when I was quite young. We hopped in the car without my brothers and headed north. We went all the way to Sacramento. I remember touring the California State Capitol and looking up into its beautiful dome for the first time. Then we went to the California State Railroad Museum. For a young boy, it was an awesome thing to be able to stand inside of an old locomotive and check out the Pullman sleeping cars. It was easy to imagine what it might have been like to travel through this great state aboard such a train. On the way home, we stopped a few times and camped, and we even fished at some small lakes. I got to be the navigator and studied the map intently, suggesting places we might check out along the way.

At the time, I did not know that this trip was not really a spur-of-the-moment endeavor to get away from the normal flow of things. This trip was intentional. It wasn't planned step by step, but it was an intentional move on my father's part to spend time with me. You see, it may be hard for you to believe, but I wasn't exactly the easiest or most obedient child. For many years, I wasn't quite sure that school was of much use at all. I thought that most rules I encountered were made to be broken, and I never seemed to go with the flow in our family.

My mom had to bear the brunt of these things. She was the one who received the phone calls from the school and the letters from my teachers. She was the one who was frustrated when the discipline didn't seem to be working at all. She was the one who broke up the fights between my older brother and me. My dad worked. He worked a lot, and things seemed to be spiraling out of control for me. So he stepped in by taking me away from all of it for a few days. Looking back, I see now that one of the blessings of my dad was that he provided a perspective that was much needed. Partially because he wasn't the one dealing with the day in, day out trials of my adolescent life, he was able to see me differently than others. Our trip to Sacramento wasn't about me getting my act together or developing a better form of discipline. As it turns out, it was about learning to see myself as my dad saw me.

Sometimes when I read St. Paul's letters to the Corinthians, I wonder how frustrated and how upset Paul must have been. Their lack of unity, their willingness to embrace false teaching, and their desires for personal glory had torn and wounded the church in Corinth. But again and again, he proclaimed to them the powerful and life-changing work of the gospel. He said, "Therefore, if anyone is in Christ he is a new creation. The old has passed away; behold, the new has come" (2 Cor. 5:17). And this new creation, this creation that was made out of the mess that was the Corinthian church, was engaged in a glorious work—a ministry of reconciliation. This work of reconciliation is the work of Christ. It is the work of the church, and by it, broken sinners are made the righteous ones of God. But who were the Corinthians to do such a thing? For that matter, we may well wonder, *who are we?*

Clearly, the work of reconciliation is an ongoing ministry of the church, which is why we gather together. We continue to preach, teach, and administer the sacraments. Through these means, God works His killing and life-giving activities, and He does so through those he has called His own dear children—through you. But our sin and our brokenness do not work only to make our efforts imperfect; they can also stifle them from ever really getting under way. The condemnation of the sin in our lives works not only to bring us to repentance but also to a place where we don't believe when our Lord says we are in Christ.

For starters, how is it that we can hope to be ministers of reconciliation when our current lives are filled with struggles? How can we focus on the care and concerns of others when we barely seem to make it through each given week ourselves? We want to be the faithful saints of God, but when we begin to examine just how it is we are doing, if we are honest with ourselves, we find that there is much to be desired in our performances. There are grudges and selfish cliques. There is disregard for the blessings of God and a willful disobedience to His commands. Our rebellion creates prisons within us, in which we are consumed with trying to make it right but are unable to do so. Around and around each of us goes, like adolescents who believe that their identities are what their frustrated teachers have labeled them to be.

But then we are given the gift of seeing ourselves through our Father's eyes. Paul, in speaking to the Corinthians, begins with a plea for endurance. This is not a plea for endurance because their lives are so stellar or because they have it all worked out. Rather, it is a plea that endurance in the grace of God finds them in their broken and hard lives. The call for endurance goes out in the face of great opposition, "in afflictions, hardships, calamities, beatings, imprisonments, riots, labors, sleepless nights, and hunger" (2 Cor. 6:4). We may well add to the list disobedient children, family struggles, and confusion about the future. But how do we endure through our afflictions?

Again, we hear the words of St. Paul. We endure "by purity, knowledge, patience, kindness, the Holy Spirit, genuine love; by truthful speech, and the power of God; with the weapons of righteousness for the right hand and the left" (2 Cor. 6:6). The tools of our endurance, the means that are needed to press on through the hardships, are not of our own making. They are the very works of the Spirit in our lives. Paul reminds us that God has placed the weapons of His righteousness in our hands. Now, we may very well wonder at the wisdom of this. We may think it's foolish that the almighty God would do such a thing. After all, when we look at one another, we see sinners unworthy to wield such weapons as the Spirit gives. But through our Father's eyes, we learn to see something more. We learn to see children clothed in the very garments of Christ.

What He sees changes everything. Again, Paul says, "We are treated as impostors, and yet are true; as unknown, and yet well known; as dying, and behold, we live; as punished, and yet not killed; as sorrowful, yet always rejoicing; as poor, yet making many rich; as having nothing, yet possessing everything" (2 Cor. 6:8–10). Out of death, our Lord brings forth life. Out of broken sinners, He makes beloved children and ambassadors of reconciliation. The cross of our Lord Jesus Christ has turned everything over.

My dad reminded me that I was more than the struggles and confusion of my young life. While he didn't ignore the wrongs I had done, he didn't allow them to define me either. In his eyes, I was something more. And for a while on that trip to Sacramento, I began to see it too. Paul encourages us all to widen our hearts and allows us to see ourselves, even for a moment, as our Father sees us. And the Father sees sins that have been atoned for. He sees the baptism that proclaimed you to be His own. He sees the words that echo in your ears, declaring that you are forgiven in Christ alone.

LIKE FATHER, LIKE SON

BOB HILLER

'm not a big fan of NASCAR. I don't fancy Formula One racing. It's not that I don't think those drivers are incredible, because I do. I would argue that racing is one of the most skilled and rigorous sports there are. I just didn't grow up with it, so it's not my thing. But while talking sports with a friend, he told me all about his love for NASCAR and Indy racing. He told me that his dad used to take him down to the race tracks and show him around the pits. He grew up on the roar of the engines, the smell of the exhaust, and the intensity of the race. He loved it, he said, because his father taught him to love it.

Though I don't share my friend's love for racing, I realized that we share something in common: our fathers handed down their love of sports to us. I've blogged before about how my love for baseball was formed by my dad. I learned how to catch, throw, and hit from my dad. He taught my brother and me how to yell at a game and overreact to inconsequential plays. For spring break, he and my mom took us to spring training and made sure we were able to attend opening day. My dad took something he loved, baseball, and passed that love on to his sons.

Of course, the Sunday after this talk was Father's Day. I'm going to guess that your church said something special about fathers. And if your church follows the lectionary, the epistle reading was probably from Galatians 3:23–4:7, in which we learn that we are adopted as children of the Heavenly Father through baptism. In the mystery of the Trinity, our Father shares an indescribable love with the Son and the Holy Spirit. He takes what, or whom, He loves (Jesus and the Spirit) and sends them to us as a gift. In baptism, God gives His children (Jew, Greek, slave, free, male, female, etc.) an inheritance purchased with the blood of Christ and the gift of the Holy Spirit, who cries out "Abba, Father" on our behalf! What is more, He does this all for free, for Christ's sake! We don't earn it by the law or any other work we might try to trust. We have an inheritance with God because Jesus purchased us with His blood by grace alone!

Now, this is an overwhelming picture of what our Father in heaven looks like, and it has a great deal to say about what it means for men to be fathers. Fathers in this world are set in place by God to be an obscure picture of God's grace. This is quite breathtaking. We dads have been given the calling to give love, mercy, and joy to our kids. We are free in Christ to demonstrate God's forgiveness when we forgive their sins. We teach them how to show mercy themselves when we confess our sins to them. We are given the overwhelming blessing of taking them to the church where we show them how to receive what matters most: Christ's gifts of word and sacrament. All of this is ours to do.

But I fear you won't hear that each Father's Day. Instead, you'll hear about how fathers are failing. You'll hear how the single most important factor in a child's faith development is the spiritual life of the father. When it comes to future church attendance, it's "like father, like son." So dads, the demise of the church is, at least in part, on you for failing to be a better man of God. Fathers will be maligned for loving their work more than their families, their laziness at home, and their immature, boyish attitudes. Then, to put a cherry on top, the service will probably end with some effeminate song designed to stir the emotions of the singers and assist everyone in falling ever more in love with their precious Jesus.

Now, as it turns out, I happen to believe that Christian families suffer because of dad's disinterested attitude toward church. But the more I hear preaching on fatherhood and the more I see the way worship is conducted, I'm not sure the blame is entirely on the fathers. Shallow, emotional music and dad shaming are about as appealing to men as a *Hallmark Channel* movie marathon.

Perhaps we could all learn how to better address fatherhood from the way Paul proclaims our Father to the Galatians. As Scott says—fathers, you are an obscure picture of our Father in heaven to your family. You are the purveyor of gifts. You are the very one God has gifted to your family to hand over the goods of forgiveness and mercy. You can show your kids how a wife should be loved. You are free to teach them to pray, study Scripture, and wrestle with the truth. You can even teach them some solid hymns! You get to be the one to pull them out of school to show them what you love. Take them to a ball game, go watch a NASCAR race, or go fishing. Even Galatians says that Christ has set us free from the schoolmaster of the law! After all, you are all sons of God, and this is how your Father in heaven treats you—by giving Jesus to die for you and sending His Spirit to dwell in your hearts. Your Father in heaven hands over the gifts. Can you even believe it? You get to share those with your family! So enjoy your freedom in Christ each Father's Day by giving your kids the goods. Like Father, like son!

FATHER KNOWS BEST

BOB HILLER

In honor of Father's Day, I want to say a few words about fatherhood. As I view the cultural landscape, I am troubled by how readily we thumb our noses at dear old Dad. We have gone from an overly idealized "father knows best" to soft-in-the-middle, bumbling Ray Barone from *Everybody Loves Raymond* in the matter of a generation. Through cultural icons such as Papa of the Berenstain Bears, the feminization of America has demoted Dad to nothing more than that sports-watching, beer-drinking, lazy waste of space that lives in front of the TV and requires Mom's mothering to survive. But fathers are gifts from the Lord. In fact, no one has a greater impact on how we view the world, our families, the church, and especially God than those men who hold the place of "father" in our lives. We need to fight against the trends that belittle fatherhood and encourage fathers to be strong, kind, and wise leaders in their homes—men who fight for their brides, provide for their children, take responsibility for their families, and are not afraid of offending those who get in their way. We need more men like my dad.

The two greatest compliments my dad ever paid me were that he thought I was a great preacher and that my little league coaches ruined my swing: "Before they adjusted your stance, you hit the ball great." You don't have to play catch with your sons to be a good dad, but we did in my house. My dad loved baseball. He still does, though he is a Rockies fan, so his love takes the form of loathing most days. My dad taught my brother and me how to catch, throw, and hit—though I won't blame him for that. There was no false distinction between quality time and quantity time with my dad as he filled my childhood with sports in the yard. When I take my kids out front with the tee and the bat, I can hear my dad's voice coming out of my mouth as I adjust their hands and correct their stance. I am in awe of how patient he was with me because I quickly get frustrated with the kids not listening to my instructions. But there his patience just gives me something to strive toward.

Since going to seminary, I've learned that balancing home and church is hard for many pastors. I didn't learn that from my dad. He was home for nearly every dinner, even when he had meetings. He made virtually all our games. And when he couldn't, it was because of an emergency. My dad knew the difference between spending time with his bride and spending time with Christ's bride. From where I sat, I never saw the latter create jealousy in the heart of the former. He was home for his family, and we knew we were his priority.

Don't get me wrong; he isn't a lazy pastor. He loves the church, and he made sure that we did too. It wasn't until two years ago that I realized that my Sunday morning routine is almost identical to my dad's. He used to wake me up early on Sundays so I could tag along as he prepared for the service. I watched as he opened the doors, turned on the lights, and made sure the sanctuary was in order for God's word to invade the lives of God's people. After telling me to leave the sanctuary so he could run through his sermon, I would peek through the window to spy on his routine. Now when I preach, especially when proclaiming the gospel, I can hear my father's voice come out of my mouth.

I'm Lutheran because my dad taught me to listen to the Scriptures alone. The poor man was burdened with a family who loved to argue theology—and we still do, in fact. He suffers sermon critiques every time my brother, who will soon have a doctorate in theology from the University of Chicago, and I, the pain-in-the-rear, come home for Christmas. One of my favorite memories is sitting down for Sunday lunch and my mom saying, "What right do we have to 'give God glory?' We can't give him anything! Why do we say it?"

My dad coolly replied, "It's in the Bible. We didn't make it up. We don't correct the Bible."

When I went through a theologically "rebellious" phase in college, I called home to tell my parents that I was leaving the Lutheran church and joining the Reformed Baptists. After all, they got baptism right. I came out to my mom first. She listened patiently, as she always does. She told me she'd tell Dad to call me when he got home. Then she called Dad immediately, as she always does. He called me within five minutes. Not being a phone guy, this was no small move. "So your mom says you aren't Lutheran anymore."

"Yeah, I just don't think it is what the Bible teaches, especially on baptism."

I made my case. I'll never forget his words: "Well, open your Bible." So now I'm a Lutheran pastor, not because my dad is one, but because my dad taught me to read the Bible.

More than anyone, fathers shape how we view God. My dad gave me a gracious picture of God. I remember sitting in fear in my basement after I had failed my first confirmation test. My mom was furious. It was the only time she ever said, "You're the pastor's son! Wait until he gets home!" I had embarrassed my dad with my laziness. I felt ashamed. He got home, stood on the stairs, and said, "What happened?"

"I failed my test."

"You think you should study harder next time?"

"Yes."

"OK. You want to watch the game?"

"Uhhh, yes!" *You want to watch the game* was as good as an absolution in my home. He never brought it up again. I learned what grace was. And for those of you who think that too much grace produces laziness, such grace prompted me to love the study of God's word as I was freed from the fear of letting my dad down.

My dad is far from perfect; he has his faults. I know them well, as I see them in my own life from time to time. But he was there. He loves his family. He trained up his boys in the way they should go. He gave us a nostalgic love for baseball and an appetite for good theology. Most importantly, he gave us Christ. I know we all want to go to heaven and have all our questions answered. But sometimes I find myself hoping that it isn't true. A heaven where I grab a beer with my dad, my brother, and my kids and argue theology around an Angel's game wouldn't be so bad.

We need more men like my dad.

THE AWESOMEST

PAUL KOCH

s a father of five, you might think that I am more of a wreck than I let on—or at least that I should be. Of course, there is the constant desire for that elusive thing called a "quiet house" or my fleeting hope to be able to take the family out to eat for under a hundred bucks (even as I endure the strange looks on the hostess's faces as they push two tables together for *all* my kids). But beyond that, there is a relentless flow of heartbreaking news that pours into our lives, places great stress on my family, and preys upon my fears as a father.

The twenty-four hour news cycles and constant updates via the Internet allow unfettered access to all the brutal and ugly things of our world. These things ought to make me worried about the future of my children. With the terror of Christians being beheaded by ISIS still in our memories, we turn the channel only to be faced with the riots in Baltimore. We turn off the TV and turn on our computers to be greeted with the horrific news of the discovery of a newborn baby's body parts found in LA County. Then, with all these images floating around my head, I sit down to dinner with my family. There, five young and (mostly) ignorant faces join my wife and me in prayer, unfazed by the insanity of it all. When I look at them, I ought to weep. I ought to be consumed with worry. I ought to be a complete wreck.

But then my five-year-old son says to me with all the confidence in the world, "Dad, you're the awesomest!"

Now, that may just sound like a funny thing a kid says about his dad. It might simply bring smiles to the faces of every father who sips their coffee out of a "#1 Dad" mug. But those words are a subtle reminder of the power of fatherhood. As I sit down to dinner with my family gathered around me, I'm not just a helpless victim of a broken world. I don't have to watch powerlessly as my children are tossed to the wolves. I'm a dad, and that is no small thing.

By design, I have far greater influence on my children than the terrors of this world do.

I can deliver strength, safety, and assurance within the home that is unmatched in our society. I can inspire revolution and obstinate resistance to the ways of our culture within the delightful anarchy of my family. In fact, even the law and the gospel are products of my words and actions long before my children learn them in church.

The problem is that we are quick to forget this power of fatherhood. We are soon convinced by the relentless shouts of the world and the many portrayals of fathers as impotent and bumbling fools so that we begin our retreat. It's not that we want to concede the field, but the deck seems stacked against us. This retreat from our position and vocation is aided by two things above all else: our own brokenness and the silence of our children.

Notice, it was my five-year-old son that said I was the awesomest and not my fifteen-year-old daughter. It's not that she wouldn't say it, but it certainly doesn't flow as effortlessly as it did when she was little. As our children grow, they also begin to trust the narrative of the world. Just as they no longer believe in the magic of their childhood when scientific explanation replaces the wonder and awe of nature, so too can the magic of their father's power and love be shaken by the disturbing realities of our culture. They also hear the cries to look elsewhere for strength and protection. They become aware of the failures of fathers. They quit reminding us of our power, for they begin to doubt it.

This abridged reminder from the lips of our children is complemented by our own brokenness. As we struggle with sin, as we fail over and again with the same old temptations and perversions, we begin to think their hushed voices are warranted. How can a man like me—a man full of doubts and fears, a man who fails more than I would ever let on, a man who feels small and helpless in the face of such opposition—change things? How can *I* change things? What can I really do in the face of such atrocities?

But then again, I am a dad.

I can shape the vision of what sort of husband my daughters will desire more than any TV show. I can show them day in, day out how a man should treat a woman. I can protect and guide better than any other force in their lives. I can teach my son more about strength and fear than the nightly news. He can learn more than knee-jerk consumerism and dead-end nihilism. He can learn honor, friendship, and compassion from me.

And here's the thing: We fathers can be this powerful force in the face of our own brokenness despite the depravity of our souls. For though our world drowns out the voices of our children, though our sin is clearly reflected in the law, we live in the love of our Father. It is a love that forgives and makes whole. It's a love that doesn't just say "It's all right" but actually does something about it. It's a love that was born, suffered, died, and rose so that you might die and rise to new life. So you are new! You are fathers bearing the love of the Father and the world cannot stop such love: "Faith, hope, and love abide, these three; but the greatest of these is love" (1 Cor. 13:13).

To put it simply, you're the awesomest!

A GOOD FATHER

PAUL KOCH

Father's Day—the day on which months of planning culminate in one large celebration. It's the day that all restaurants are booked and any last-minute details are finalized so that families can come together and finally tell their fathers how much they love them. Well, perhaps the plans are never that extravagant and the restaurants are never booked, but most dads that I know are fine with that reality. We know full well that as far as days of celebration go, Father's Day is a far cry from Mother's Day. We know that it wasn't even an established national holiday until Nixon signed it into law in 1977, some sixty years after Mother's Day.

However, the first recorded celebration of Father's Day is a story worth retelling. In Fairmont, West Virginia all the way back on 1908, a day was set aside to focus on the gift of fathers. It came in the wake of the greatest mining disaster in the history of the United States. An explosion at the Fairmont Coal Company in nearby Monongah damaged the ventilation systems along with the railcars and support timbers in the mines. The inability to clear the mines of toxic gas quickly turned the rescue effort into a recovery effort. All in all, 362 men died in those mines, leaving 250 women widows and more than a thousand children fatherless. That first Father's Day was an attempt to honor their memory, to weep and mourn and give thanks for the gift of fatherhood.

This somber beginning to Father's Day gives it a remorseful and longing flavor. And I think that is fitting. Deep within all of us is a longing for one of the most powerful forces known to man—a good father. A good father establishes our identities and provides what is needed. He is there to protect, guide, and love. Those who have a good father know the treasure that they have and fear losing it. And those who don't have a good father, or any father at all, long for that which they have missed in their life. Like a distant echo, there is this faint remnant of what ought to be there but they can't find. And I have never met a father who doesn't want to be a good father. They aren't all good, even against their own expectations, but somehow they still measure themselves against a standard of a good father.

This longing for a good father is taken up by St. Paul as we continue through his letter to the Galatians. He has chastised them for their wayward ways; their desire is to take up the law again as a measure of their faithfulness and base of their salvation. He has done the work again of killing and bringing forth new life as they are emptied of their own work and filled with the life and gifts of Christ himself. He has made the bold declaration that you have been crucified with Christ and it is no longer you who lives but Christ who lives in you. This new life then changes your identity; you are not what you were before. You are the sons of God, and your Father is truly a good father.

"Sons of God" is a delightful title to have. Now, you may want the title to be "children of God," or at least "sons and daughters of God." But a son of God is a very particular title, a title that encompasses the young and old, men and women, Jew and Gentile alike. When the Lord sent Moses back to Egypt to demand that Pharaoh let his people go, He said to Moses, "You shall say to Pharaoh, 'Thus says the Lord, Israel is my firstborn son, and I say to you, let my son go that he may serve me" (Exod. 4:22). Israel is God's son—the whole nation, young and old, male and female.

They are His son. They are heirs of His blessings and protected and loved by God. It was their identity. It gave meaning and purpose to their existence.

But then, thousands of years later, Jesus of Nazareth stood in the waters of the Jordan River to be baptized by John to fulfill all righteousness. There, the Lamb of God, who takes away the sins of the world, repented for sins that were not his own. He repented for the sins he would bear to the cross—for your sins. As he was washed in them, the heavens opened up and the eternal Father declared, "This is my beloved Son, with whom I am well pleased" (Matt. 3:17). Israel, God's son, wandered away from their good Father. They had turned their back on the gracious Father who loved them and called them by name. But in those waters that lead ultimately to the cross of Calvary and the empty tomb was the good Son, the faithful son, the Son that wouldn't reject the blessings of the Father, the Son that would endure the punishment others had earned so that his Father might have mercy on them.

As Israel's identity was found in the love of their Father and Christ's identity is found in his perfect service of the Father, so you are now called the sons of God. You are the inheritors of the blessings and mercy secured by the true and eternal Son of God. You are those chosen and set apart to be his children. You have received the adoption as sons. Paul says, "Because you are sons, God has sent the Spirit of his Son into our hearts, crying, 'Abba! Father!'" (Gal. 4:6). Our longing for a good father is made complete in our adoption into the eternal family of God.

It's important to note that this new identity as the sons of God comes by adoption. Adoption doesn't work by our effort or will. Adoption isn't a product of our best PR campaign. Adoption is completely the work of another. It is an external word that declares something about who we are. In other words, God didn't just get stuck with you. It's not that he wasn't without options as far as children go. And it's not that you did something at the right time and in the right way to earn your adoption. And so, the sonship first given to Israel and then perfected in the love of Christ is now freely given to you.

According to Paul, the law was our guardian before the gift of faith in Christ. The law oversaw our comings and goings until we were declared to be heirs of the kingdom of God, free in the love of our Father. In the waters of Holy Baptism, you die, your sins are exposed, and your shame is revealed. But you are not left for dead. For you rise from those waters filled with new life, with new breath, and with a new identity. You are the sons of God. "For as many of you as were baptized into Christ have put on Christ. There is neither Jew nor Greek, there is neither slave nor free, there is neither male nor female, for you are all one in Christ Jesus" (Gal. 3:27).

This adoption into the household of faith is a transformative thing. You may live out your days struggling and wondering who you really are. You may have doubts about how to plan for your future or confusion about what the best career path is. You might be fearful about retirement and what it means for the next stage of life. You might be near the bedside of someone you love who won't be around for much longer. And what you will need more than anything else—what you must have to endure and to press on—is a father, a good father who will protect, guide, comfort, and forgive you.

You have that Father. His own Spirit resides within you, crying out in times of joy and sadness, confusion and hope to a Father who will not forsake you, nor abandon you, nor leave you in darkness. Rather, he speaks a ceaseless word to his sons. He speaks a word to the men and women of his family, to the young and old, the Jews and Gentiles. It is the same word that all earthly fathers need to hear and the same word they long to speak. It is a simple word, but it's powerful. It is the word of our good Father, who says to you, "I forgive you, I love you, you are mine today and forevermore."

FATHER FAILS
AND FORGIVENESS

ROSS ENGEL

My wife once commented that my sermons had been overflowing with forgiveness. But before I could thank her for such a great compliment, she asked me, "Have you been needing more forgiveness lately?"

The truth of the matter is that I always need forgiveness—lots of it! We all do. Sinners to the very core are always in need of forgiveness.

> *It is a trustworthy statement, deserving full acceptance, that Christ Jesus came into the world to save sinners, among whom I am foremost of all. Yet for this reason I found mercy, so that in me as the foremost, Jesus Christ might demonstrate His perfect patience as an example for those who would believe in Him for eternal life. (1 Tim. 1:15–16)*

This time, the words of forgiveness that I needed to hear came from my three- and five-year-old daughters.

After a particularly long day, I blew my top, lost my patience, and raised my voice. I was ticked off. I could probably justify my anger. After all, it was bedtime. My two girls were supposed to be cleaning up their room, getting their PJs on, and doing their bedtime routine. Instead, they were monkeying around in their underwear. I'm not exactly sure what they were up to, but dad was not happy.

Typically, my girls are good at following instructions. Though only children, they do a good job doing what they're asked to do and are self-sufficient when it comes to their daily tasks. But for some reason, they were all out of sorts. I guess I was too.

Through angry, tear-filled eyes, my oldest daughter looked at me and said, "Daddy, we're not monkeying around, and we're not a bunch of knuckleheads . . ."

Yeah, I had a father fail. I got angry and told my girls that they were "acting like a bunch of knuckleheads."

The rest of the bedtime routine of books, prayers, and a song were punctuated with the sniffling of little girls' tears. The girls went to bed sad, and I sat in my study wishing that I had done things differently and that I hadn't lost my patience so spectacularly. As I sat in my little pity party, I realized that I won't be my children's hero for long if they are terrified of me and want nothing to do with me.

But like the Psalmist says, "Joy comes in the morning" (Ps. 30:5).

At breakfast, my girls and I talked about the night before. They apologized for their behavior, and I forgave them. And as they chowed down on their cereal, I then asked them to forgive me for losing my patience and for calling them a pair of knuckleheads. Both girls jumped quickly out of their chairs, ran to me, and said, "We forgive you, Daddy." Forgiveness was delivered, hugs and kisses were exchanged, and the day began with gladness and reconciliation. The bond between father and daughters was repaired!

How blessed is he whose transgression is forgiven, whose sin is covered! (Ps. 32:1)

When I talk with others about forgiveness, I often use the example of a father forgiving his children and how children experience great peace and joy when a parent forgives them of their wrongdoing. When children are in trouble, they often carry with them a lot of fear. They can find themselves wondering if their relationship—their place in the family—is at risk because of something they did wrong. Forgiveness gives them the assurance that they are still a welcomed part of the family and that they have not messed up enough that they're no longer a beloved child. It works the other way too. Hearing those words of forgiveness from my two daughters assured me that I hadn't failed so badly that my girls had written me off or turned their backs on me as their dad.

I'm not the perfect dad. My wife and kids might be the first ones to admit that. But even when I mess up, confession and absolution pull me out of the despair of all my father fails.

When it comes to our Heavenly Father, confession and absolution are what release us from the burden our sins place upon us. God has every right to be angry with us for our failings, shortcomings, and sins. Yet He has graciously promised that when we confess our sins to Him, He forgives us and cleanses us from all our unrighteousness. Sins are placed on Jesus, the debt is paid, and Christ delivers His righteousness to His people.

I need that kind of forgiveness every day. What a joyous thing it is that God continues to deliver that gift of forgiveness to each of us!

PART FOUR
FRIENDSHIP

∧ IT'S OK THAT WE'RE
NOT FRIENDS . . .
I LIKE IT THAT WAY!

FINDING ∧
MY BROTHER

GUNS, BEER, ∧
AND BIBLICAL
TRANSLATION

∧ DANGEROUS
FRIENDSHIPS

IN THE COMPANY ∧
OF GREAT MEN

∧ A GATHERING
OF MEN

∧ THE NAMES
I'VE FORGOTTEN

∧ MUTUAL BROTHERLY
CONSOLATION AND
FORGIVENESS

THE REBELLION ∧
OF FRIENDSHIP

∧ THE JOY OF SEX
AND CHURCH

∧ WELCOME TO
THE REBELLION

∧
I AM FRODO
BAGGINS

∧ FRIENDSHIP

IT'S OK THAT WE'RE NOT FRIENDS . . . I LIKE IT THAT WAY!

SCOTT KEITH

> To the Ancients, Friendship seemed the happiest and most fully human of all loves; the crown of life and the school of virtue. The modern world, in comparison ignores it.
>
> —C. S. LEWIS, *THE FOUR LOVES*

Once again, the Kochs and the Keiths were at O'Leary's bar drinking a few cocktails, and the conversation turned to friendship. Maybe it's because we are good friends or because we like to wax philosophical, but conversations like this always come up. As often happens, it was the lovely and talented Mrs. Koch and I who were seemingly butting heads. At one point, she bluntly asked me, "So what does it mean to be a true friend?" As she asked her question, it occurred to me that I ask this question of myself quite a lot. I don't have many friends. I often wonder if that is because I am unlikable—it probably is—or if it is for some other reason. I know many people who have more friends than they can count. But when I'm around them, I always feel like I'm in that scene from *Tombstone* in which Wyatt Earp asks Doc Holiday to stay in bed and out of his fight. In a weak attempt to explain himself, Doc Holiday says, "Wyatt Earp is my friend." To which one of the posse quickly retorts, "Hell, I got lots of friends." What comes next from Doc always hits me right between the eyes as he exclaims, "I don't." I don't either.

Friendship involves a care, commitment, and desire toward the same "higher order" of things in life. If we are friends, it says more than that we share a common interest. Friends walk side by side with one another on the path of life that yearns toward discovering quality, meaning, and virtue. Friends share a desire to seek after what is right and what ought to be. Friends stand together, facing the world in its complexities and nuances, attempting to make sense of it and encounter it together. In his work *The Four Loves*, C. S. Lewis says that lovers are usually pictured facing one another and friends are pictured walking side by side. Within the confines of a romantic relationship or a marriage, the relationship itself is often the subject of conversation. Sure, these people are dedicated to each other, might be friends, and hopefully would do anything for one another, but they are lovers. Thus their relationship focuses on their love for one another. The focus of a friendship is never the friendship itself. In a very particular way, friendship is deeper than that. Friends work toward those things that are outside of us that bring value and virtue to our existence. Lovers will make love, but friends will be doing something outside of themselves together.

You see, we can't be friends. I don't know you. We have no common interest, nothing that we can work toward together, no philosophical conundrum to work out. We might not even be acquaintances. To you, I am likely merely words on a page, with which you may agree or disagree.

In many ways, friendship demands more of us than any other type of relationship. It requires that we find someone with whom we can share adventures of either the mind or the body. Thus it requires work. Referring to digital friends as such is insulting to the concept of friendship. It's not possible to walk alongside a computer screen and create the subversion of the larger group that is inevitable when two friends remove themselves from the herd to work out the mysteries of life. No greater virtue exists, and it is a virtue only found among friends.

Friendship is not necessary to life, but it makes life worth living. Again, C. S. Lewis is helpful as he says it this way: "Friendship is unnecessary like philosophy, like art, like the universe itself (for God did not need to create). It has no survival value; rather, it is one of those things that give value to survival" (Lewis, *The Four Loves*). It is more virtuous to have fewer true friends to walk alongside of on the journey of life than to have many acquaintances in the clothing of friendship that don't fit the bill. The virtue is achieved by two souls seeking after those things that make this life valuable to live. A true friend is an incredibly valuable commodity. What makes something valuable is that it is in short supply. What makes diamonds and gold valuable is that they are hard to mine. Friends are also hard to mine, so they are valuable. So you are most likely not my friend, and that's OK. We ought to both like it that way because it means we have true friends.

FINDING MY BROTHER

PAUL KOCH

For he today that sheds his blood with me / Shall be my brother . . .
—WILLIAM SHAKESPEARE, *HENRY V*

I had a T-shirt in college with that line on it. I had no idea that it was penned by Shakespeare. I didn't know it was from the famous St. Crispin's Day speech from *Henry V* or that the actual battle of Agincourt in 1415 inspired the scene. However, without a doubt, I knew the truth of the words.

I bought the shirt at a rugby tournament. Now, I could go on and on about the beauty and joy of the game of rugby, but the truth is, it's also a violent and brutal sport. To walk onto the pitch, line up next to those other men, and engage in what is a sort of controlled warfare for sport was to find a brotherhood unlike much else outside of true war. To bleed alongside those men, to fight, scrape, and lay it all on the line with men I hardly knew just a few minutes before, changed things. They had my back and I had theirs. During the blood, sweat, and dirt, everyone found a brother.

I miss that brotherhood. I miss it in that deep pit in my stomach in a way that is hard to articulate. It makes me long for the violence of that comradery.

I played rugby for fifteen years. I accumulated delightful scars, sang horribly offensive songs, and had my masculinity checked over and over again. What I thought I was owed or believed I was worth didn't mean shit unless I could back it up on the field. There was a clear external and objective physicality to a man's place in things on a rugby team. And yet, at the moment of the kickoff that signaled the beginning of the battle—from the fiercest man to the most pathetic—they became brothers willing to bleed for one another. And whoever was not willing, backing away from the fray, would be pushed out of the comradeship with shocking speed. Rugby was hard on the body. It was violent and jarring. Yet I long for those days. I long for them like a heartbroken boy longs for his first summer love.

But why? Do I miss lacing up heavy braces on my ankles just to make it through another match? Not really. Do I miss the taste of my own blood in my mouth after taking a knee to the face in the bottom of a ruck? A little, perhaps. Do I miss the opportunity to prove myself? Sure, I think so, but I have found other ways to do that. What I really miss and truly long for are my brothers.

Rugby and the men I played with were a constant check against the pseudomasculinity of our current Facebook culture, in which everyone crafts their own commercials of themselves. Somehow, having brothers who would willingly bleed alongside me helped me to understand my place in the world. They were the physical reminders of Tyler Durden in *Fight Club* saying, "You are not your job. You're not how much money you have in the bank. You are not the car you drive. You're not the contents of your wallet. You are not your f@*ing khakis." So when I lost my brothers, I lost something of myself.

Back when Scott was working on his book *Being Dad*, I would often spend some time with him in a few choice dive bars in Ventura, talking about life, theology, and our unreasonable desire to sing Kenny Rogers when we've had just one drink too many. But one area of life that we would regularly talk about was masculinity, friendship, and what it took to raise a boy to become a man in our current culture. Somewhere there, if either expressly articulated or simply understood as an unspoken truth, was the necessity of brothers. In a world in which masculinity is either shamed as the dying vestige of a misogynistic culture or mutated into a Calvin Klein underwear ad, there is no anchor for a man to be a man outside of other men. But perhaps this has always been so.

Those conversations and the success of his book inspired me to try something that might function to help me find my brothers again. I simply invited some men to gather together to talk, to share their stories of struggle, failure, and victory. After closing hours, once a month, a cool little camera shop in our town opens for a gathering of men. Most of the men are fathers, some married and some divorced, but all know that there is something missing that they are longing to find again. We tell stories about how we've let down our own fathers and how we've made them proud. We've discussed what defines the essence of a man and what it is to be a protector and provider. We talk about our fears and revel in the insane confidence that our sons will rise to the occasion and succeed where we have failed. There is something so refreshing and powerful about this time together. To hear other men tell their stories is a reminder that we are not alone.

Through it all, I began to find what I feared was lost—brothers, not bound together in the blood and sweat of the rugby pitch, but bound together in the flesh and blood of real life. As we share our stories, we find that nervous laughter of the commercial façade gives way to the hearty laughter of men who will stand beside us in battle. In fact, I think it is accurate to say that we've been in the battle all along. We just didn't know who was standing next to us until now.

"Iron sharpens iron, and one man sharpens another," says Solomon. That sharpening may not always be pleasant. It may leave scars along the way. But deep within, it is a love that is unshakable even when victory is far from certain.

"We few, we happy few, we band of brothers;
For he to-day that sheds his blood with me

Shall be my brother; be he ne'er so vile,
This day shall gentle his condition;
And gentlemen in England now a-bed
Shall think themselves accurs'd they were not here,
And hold their manhoods cheap whiles any speaks
That fought with us upon Saint Crispin's day."

Henry V (Act IV, Scene iii)

GUNS, BEER, AND BIBLICAL TRANSLATION

PAUL KOCH

Every Tuesday morning, I meet up with three other pastors from my circuit to translate the lessons for the upcoming Sunday. Now, this may seem like a simple task, but I assure you, it is not. This habit has had a profound impact on my vocation. It has challenged me, caused me to focus, and even helped me to stay out of trouble a few times. Ideas are batted back and forth between texts as we revel in that great mixture of insults and encouragement at which men of almost any age seem to naturally excel.

But these weekly gatherings are not simple, practical meetings to achieve a set goal. They have a certain unpredictability about them that manages to keep us always desiring to begin our workweek in the company of each other.

As an example, consider one of our gatherings. Jon and I arrived early because I asked Tim if he would hear my confession before we began our meeting. Tim shut and locked the doors to his study and we followed the order from the *Pastoral Care Companion* for the rite of individual confession and absolution. I took a deep breath and said, "Pastor, please hear my confession and pronounce forgiveness to fulfill God's will." Within moments, I found myself feeling awkward and foolish as I said things out loud that made me feel ashamed and ugly. In the end, Tim placed his hands upon my head and forgave me in the name of the Father, the Son, and the Holy Spirit and set me free in Christ.

After that, I slid a small gun case across the table to Tim. Now, I don't know much at all about guns. Tim does, however, and as a former San Diego police officer, he has the training and knowledge to back it up. He had been trying to get me to go to the range with him. I was really looking forward to it, but until then, I wanted him to look at something. Years ago, I was given one of my wife's grandfather's guns, a small Beretta that he brought home from World War II. Long story short, by the time Jon came back into the room, Tim was enthusiastically examining a firearm, leaving Jon to think that either the confession went well or was about to go very wrong.

No sooner had Tim packed away the gun than Matt showed up dragging a small keg behind him. Remember, this was supposed to be a time for translation work. It turned out that his church had just finished an Octoberfest celebration. There was part of a small keg from Island Brewing Company left over, so he brought it to share.

There we were, gathered around a small table while sipping on beer as we worked our way through 2 Timothy, laughing at each other's mistakes and coming up with great ideas that we will probably never even try to bring to fruition. From Tim's study, we headed down to our usual lunch spot for the wonder that is Taco Tuesday. More laughs and fun ensued from certain decisions that were not well thought out. In the end, while heading back to Ventura with Jon, we had a conversation about manhood and his fears and excitement in anticipation of his first child.

And as I think about it, I realize that this "shocking" day wasn't all that shocking or unusual. Our translation time doesn't always come with guns and beer kegs, but it's as if it was never out of the question that it could happen. And it is this that I find fascinating.

I remember a former professor of mine saying that a fellowship is only worth what it fellowships around. It's what stands at the center of a fellowship that gives that fellowship its meaning and strength. For my little group of brothers on Tuesday mornings, the one thing that is never in question is what we gather around. We gather around the word.

Everything else—from laughs over tacos to confession and absolution—flows from the word at the center. What I find that I am always learning to receive is the organic consequence of a living word of God. That word that we approach in Greek and Hebrew with second-guesses and trembling hands is not relegated to a compartment in our lives. Rather, it infiltrates us, tears down walls of separation, and allows for trust and hope to bloom. The word gives me the confidence to speak my sins aloud, expect absolution, and share a cold beer and make plans for a subtle takeover of the synod.

It is this same word that gathers us together in worship and establishes and breathes life into the church. It's not just a compartment within your life, not just something you do on Sunday morning and then set aside. When you gather around the word, you gather around something that is dynamic and powerful. This word can give you a sure footing and solid foundation on the one hand and free you to do joyful and amazing things on the other. It binds you to brothers and sisters from whom you can expect confession and absolution. And if you're lucky, perhaps you can even expect some tacos.

IN THE COMPANY OF GREAT MEN

SCOTT KEITH

'm lucky whenever I have the chance to spend time in the company of great men. I often ponder the importance of spending time with men who are smarter and wiser than I am. I feel that it is something that is devalued in our contemporary ideology. As I perceive the contemporary view concerning "learning from one's elders," what I hear is that those who are older are rarely better, mostly out of touch, and almost always in need of updated information. Yet I'm not sure this is the case.

Consider the case of Albert Matye. Albert was my great-uncle, the brother of my grandfather, Walter. Albert died in 2009 at the age of ninety-four. In my estimation, he was a great man. Albert was not what many would have considered even a good man in his formative years. He was an alcoholic and a cad by all accounts. He cleaned up in his fifties, and it was from that point forward that I knew him as my Uncle Al. He lived in Moro Bay, California, and we would make trips to his home every summer when I was a boy. I remember sitting at his feet, listening to him talk, and watching him work in his garden and his woodshop. As I grew older, some of these times drifted away. I didn't think I had much to learn from Uncle Al anymore. When I was in my late twenties, I moved our family to northern Nevada, and it just happened that where we now lived was no more than ten miles from Uncle Al's new house in Minden. I would see him every holiday and birthday. He was the great-grandpa that my kids never had, and he was the grandpa I hadn't had in some twenty years. I learned about politics, religion, philosophy, history, and even life in general from my Uncle Al. His words and perspectives were not those of a scholar but of a man who had lived hard and learned how to be a good man the hard way. I can't imagine what a different man I would be today if I had continued to despise his counsel rather than embrace his wisdom.

The most wonderful part of this past trip for me was the time I was blessed to spend with Dr. Rod Rosenbladt and Dr. James A. Nestingen at Dr. Nestingen's home in Oregon. Dr. Rosenbladt was my mentor through my undergraduate years at Concordia University Irvine, and Dr. Nestingen was my doctoral thesis supervisor. But much more than that, these men are my friends, and I am lucky to have them. In my estimation, they are great men.

From Dr. Rosenbladt, I learned all things theological, philosophical, and at times, even political. But more than that, I learned that a man is gracious and kind, strong through his forgiveness not his muscles, and always puts his children first. In short, I learned much of what it means to be a good man and a good father. This is not to say or imply that I always live up to those lessons. Rather, because I have been in the company of this great man, I know where to look for love and forgiveness when I fail. He is my friend and a great man.

What I have learned from Dr. Nestingen is inestimable. He was not so much my theological teacher as he was my refiner. He took my sharp edges (and they were sharp!) and softened them with grace, graciousness, and the forgiveness won for us in Christ. He refined my understanding of the true importance of properly distinguishing the law from the gospel. He helped me understand that there is truly no power stronger than that of the preached gospel of Christ. He mentored me concerning marriage and what it means to be a kind and caring husband. (I still need this mentorship and more.) He is my friend and a great man.

Spending time on the porch smoking and drinking with these two men and learning from their conversations with one another was more than that which I am worthy. We drank wonderful Aquavit, ate a blessed meal prepared by Carolyn Nestingen, and smoked tasty tobacco from beautiful pipes. Together, we discussed my work and their influences on me. We reminisced in our mutual friendship and love for one another. I listened closely as they discussed theology, theological movements and influences, personalities, mutual friendships and acquaintances, politics, friendship in general, and the freedom of the gospel. Once again, I learned from them what true male friendship looks like. I learned again about the company of great men.

Men need to learn from other men. Many of you may remember from my previous blog posts that I am a fan of the work *Iron John* by Robert Bly. Bly has much to say regarding the relationships that are necessary between men. I picked it up again today and ran across a passage that I underlined: "In ordinary life, a mentor can guide a young man through various disciplines, helping to bring him out of boyhood into manhood; and that in turn is associated not with body building, but with the building of an emotional body capable of containing more than one sort of ecstasy. We know, moreover, that such initiation does not take place at any one moment or only once" (Bly, *Iron John*, 233).

These men are not great because they are any better or worse than other sinners in this world. They are not. I think I know them well enough to say that they, like you and me, are the worst of sinners. They sin in thought, word, and deed. The blood of the Lamb redeems them, and that is what makes them great. What makes them great to me is that they were willing to share with me who they are in Christ—not just once but time and time again in every moment they had to spare. All men need to be in the company of great men. I hope you have some great men in your life. If you don't, find some. If others around you don't, consider trying to be a great man to them.

DANGEROUS FRIENDSHIPS

SCOTT KEITH

I recently finished the C. S. Lewis biography authored by Alister McGrath entitled *C. S. Lewis—a Life: Eccentric Genius, Reluctant Prophet*. I highly recommend it. Over the weekend, I also attended The Great Conversation (TGC) C. S. Lewis symposium. At the symposium, Diana Pavlac Glyer, professor of English at Azusa Pacific University, gave a talk on the influence of the Inklings on the thoughts of C. S. Lewis. I am struck by the extent to which great writers like Lewis and Tolkien seemed to use what McGrath calls "midwives" when writing their great works. Or as Glyer put it, "We all need dangerous friends" (Glyer, "Creative Opposition").

Many of you may not be familiar with the Inklings. The Inklings were an informal literary circle in Oxford that began meeting in the early 1930s and continued until the late 1940s. The core of the group consisted of C. S. Lewis and J. R. R. Tolkien. They took pleasure in listening to one another read their works in progress aloud. Lewis and Tolkien invited other well-known, and not so well-known, authors to join them for informal, convivial meetings in Oxford pubs—later adding evening gatherings—to read their works aloud, receiving both praise and candid criticism.

Gradually, the schedule of Inklings' meetings became regularized, so they generally met on Tuesday mornings at the Eagle and Child pub (which they called the "Bird and Baby" or just the "Bird") and on Thursday evenings at Lewis's study rooms in Magdalen College, where he was an Oxford don. At the pub, they smoked their pipes, drank, and had good food, almost like hobbits. While they sat at the bar, they talked about language and literature. Others in the group included Owen Barfield, Warren Lewis, Nevill Coghill, Hugo Dyson, and Charles Williams.

As described by those in the know, the Inklings were not afraid to mix it up a bit. These men were not alike. Lewis was brash and boisterous. Tolkien seems to have been more reserved and introspective. They did not agree on many things. Tolkien is said to have believed that Lewis's use of allegory in his *Ransom* trilogy and the *Chronicles of Narnia* was perhaps too obvious. In fact, they often disagreed on issues of morality. McGrath explains that Tolkien believed that Lewis's view concerning civil marriage was against the teaching of the church. Thus the evidence points to the fact that Tolkien disapproved of Lewis's marriage to Joy Davidman.

Despite these differences, they still met. They took the time to meet because friendship, creativity, and debate are important. They acknowledged that friendship, especially male friendship, does not work when it is focused on the other friend. As Lewis says in *The Four Loves*, friends walk alongside each other and together cast their gaze at something outside themselves. In our current cultural milieu, this is a dangerous idea. When we cast our gaze on something else, some other topic, some other work, or some other concept, we open ourselves to the possibility of disagreement. Conversations between real friends are dangerous in that while friends walk alongside one another, their time is often spent in heated debate about the object of their conversation.

I think we need to regain some of these dangerous friendships. We need friendships like what Lewis and Tolkien shared.

A friendship of this kind is defined by at least two people taking the initiative and making the time to share, care, and listen to the ideas of the other. This listening will then often turn into examination and critique of the ideas being proposed. In due time, examination and critique will result in debate over the ideas. Debate is where the danger arises, but it is also where we experience iron sharpening iron. As the proverb says, "Iron sharpens iron, and one man sharpens another" (Prov. 27:17).

To accomplish this, we need friends who are not like us. When being a midwife to the work of another, the work cannot be what we would have produced ourselves. Recent data suggests that our brains grow when we are paired in creative enterprise with another person. When we converse and create together, we become better.

I think it can be argued, and I am not alone, that the Inklings were effective as a group because of their intellectual and personality differences. As Lewis explains in *An Experiment in Criticism*, there is not one person among us who holds all the great ideas. The creative process seems to demand that we develop friendships with people who are not like us, that we be hungry for rational opposition. This rational opposition forms the basis of what Glyer coined "intellectual hospitality," which in turn builds the foundations of great friendships.

Glyer began her paper by saying, "If you want to be like Lewis, you need a little more Tolkien in your life" (Glyer, "Creative Opposition"). Though the two men were friends, they did have a falling-out of sorts in the late 1940s. To my way of thinking, this only shows that they were both sinners, not that they weren't friends. The proof of their enduring mutual friendship and respect comes later. In 1961, long after the Inklings had been disbanded, Lewis nominated Tolkien for the Nobel Prize in Literature for his benchmark work, *The Lord of the Rings*. Tolkien did not win the prize, but Lewis's nomination of his friend shows that he never lost respect for his friend nor his sense of intellectual hospitality.

I would like to be more like Lewis. Therefore, I think I need a little more Tolkien in my life. Any takers?

A GATHERING
OF MEN

SCOTT KEITH

The first time I was asked to present the content of *Being Dad*, in an interesting moment of serendipity, was at the place where I first began teaching, Faith Lutheran Church in Capistrano Beach. Every month, Faith hosts a men's movie night. The evening is an opportunity for the men of the church to get together, drink, smoke, hang out, watch a movie, and just be men together. This night, instead of watching a movie, I presented concepts of gracious fatherhood, friendship, and meaningful mentoring.

For me, this night was truly magical, not because of myself or the subject matter of my teaching, but because of the other men. After I had taught for about an hour, I opened the floor up for questions. The questions that came were, as is often the case, given to me more in the form of comments than questions. Some were about how wonderful it was to be in the company of other men discussing the need for the presence of more strong men.

Our culture begrudges the presence of masculine men. Our cultural milieu would not tell us that masculinity is a laudable trait. Watching television, going to the movies, and engaging in the contemporary culture through modern media tell us that almost every man is homosexual, impotent, stupid, incapable, or irrelevant. This is the opposite of what I experienced at this session. Rather, I experienced a group of men who were strong, capable, kind, gracious, magnanimous, and supportive. Pastors, professors, teachers, scientists, lawyers, and engineers, all of them were alike—masculine men.

Though I hardly knew many of the men present, I was reminded again that masculine men have a true sense of brotherly friendship and love, or *philia*. That is why every time I find myself surrounded by other masculine men, I know that I am in a safe place. Therefore, I say in *Being Dad*, "It sometimes seems that masculine men run in herds because they are often together. It is not some sort of gang mentality; rather, it is iron sharpening iron. In the ancient world, *philia* was the most praiseworthy of all forms of love. *Friendship* was to the ancients seen as the cornerstone of the development of virtue, while our modern world, by way of contrast, completely disregards it. In our social media–encumbered world, there are few who find virtue in true friendship. Few find *virtue* in friendship because few have actually experienced real masculine friendship for themselves" (Keith, *Being Dad*).

Men need to be in the company of other men. Young men need to be in the company of older men and the other way around. In *Iron John*, the great American poet Robert Bly quotes Wordsworth from *The Excursion*:

> *He loved me; from a swarm of rosy boys*
> *Singled me out, as he in sport would say,*
> *For my grave looks, too thoughtful for my years.*
> *As I grew up, it was my best delight*
> *To be his chosen comrade. Many a time*
> *On holidays, we wandered through the woods . . .*

Bly goes on to elaborate the problem of our day: "Much of that chance incidental mingling has ended. Men's clubs and societies have disappeared. Grandfathers live in Phoenix or the old people's home, and many boys experience only the companion-ship of other boys their age who, from the point of view of the old initiators, know nothing at all" (Bly, *Iron John*, 16).

When I "happen" to fall into evenings like this one, I am often tempted to believe that such an event happened by chance. I'm not sure my idea of *chance* is properly a Christian idea. In fact, I think C. S. Lewis would disagree strongly. In *The Four Loves*, Lewis says, "But, for a Christian, there are, strictly speaking, no chances. A secret Master of the Ceremonies has been at work. Christ, who said to the disciples 'Ye have not chosen me, but I have chosen you,' can truly say to every group of Christian friends 'You have not chosen one another, but I have chosen you for one another.' Friendship is not a reward for discrimination and good taste in finding one another out. It is the instrument by which God reveals to each the beauties of all the others."

Many men don't know how wonderful the company of other men can be. Some literally don't even know what the word *man* means or, as Bly says, whether they are grown men or not. For me, I need to thank Faith Lutheran Church for opportunities like this gathering. Every time I am granted entrance into the company of other men—gracious and masculine men—I know what Lewis felt when he said, "There's no sound I like better than the sound of male laughter" (Lewis, *The Four Loves*). In that laughter and in the company of other men, I find the grace of God at work on me, coming to me in the loving assurance of gracious, masculine men.

Bly claimed, "It's important to be able to say the word *mascu-line* without imagining that we are saying a sexist word" (Bly, *Iron John*). If we believe that being masculine and surrounding our-selves with other masculine men is sexist, we will never accept that we need these men in our lives. This would be a great trag-edy. As men, we need other men to be our iron sharpening iron, our oasis from the world at war with us, to share with us a sense of true *philia* and to be the word of grace and forgiveness on the lips of others.

THE NAMES
I'VE FORGOTTEN

SCOTT KEITH

> The one who conquers will be clothed thus in white garments, and I will never blot his name out of the book of life. I will confess his name before my Father and before his angels.
>
> —REV. 3:5

During one of our final dinners of our trip to England, we somehow wandered to the topic of old friends. We were discussing friends we had in common and those with whom we had lost touch. At one point in our conversation, the name of my friend Justin came up and I was, almost inexplicably, brought to tears. I have written of my profound sadness concerning Justin previously. What caused me to despair this time is that, from then until now, I have hardly thought of Justin. You see, it is as if I had forgotten his name. One of the great tragedies of Justin's time on this earth is the reality that so many people, including me, were all too willing to forget his name.

I was not ready for what occurred to me next. As tears rolled down my face, I began to remember all the names of those I have known and loved whose names I have, for all intents and purposes, forgotten—friends like Kevin and Justin, grandparents like Walter, Jean, Lottie-Gene, and Paul, and my father-in-law, Ted. In my sin, I even tend to forget the name of my own father, Charles Leonard Keith. My memory is weak and my will weaker.

These people were everything to me at one time or another. In the darkness of my sin, I cannot even muster the energy or integrity to remember their names as I walk through this day-to-day life. For a moment of time, the guilt that this sudden realization produced in me was quite overwhelming. How could I forget about my friends, my grandparents, or my father for even a short time? I lose sight because I am usually too concerned with myself to consider others. In a perverse twist of irony, this whole exercise of trying to remember those who have gone before me was beginning to turn into my personal pity party regarding my weakness.

Then I remembered something that we all lose track of all too quickly. The legacy of those who have gone before us is not defined by our memory of them. Rather, it is established in Christ's memory. If they have died in Him, He has placed their names in His book of life, and He will never forget them. What is more, He promises that He will confess their names before the Father and before His angels. Here is the sure sign and the sure hope of those that are in Christ.

I like to try to make most things about me; I suspect you are the same. Life seems easier when we find something for which we can take the blame. In an odd sort of way, it is almost harder to express that my memory of my father's name matters so much less than Christ's memory of his name. But my hope in meeting my earthly father some day in paradise will only be fulfilled because Christ has remembered his name and placed it in His book of life, not because I have or have not diligently guarded his memory and legacy.

What a glorious Savior we have! He knows our every weakness and fulfills our every need. He fills the holes of our empty lives with purpose through the redemption He has showered upon us through His atoning death and life-giving resurrection. He has made war against the powers of sin, death, and the devil and has become victorious for us. He takes our flawed memories and replaces our memorial weaknesses with His unfailing promise, "I will confess his name before my Father and before his angels."

In the future, I will probably continue to fret when I realize that I have once more forgotten the names of those who have gone before me. But next time, the words of our Lord will come more freely to my lips: "The one who conquers will be clothed thus in white garments, and I will never blot his name out of the book of life. I will confess his name before my Father and before his angels" (Rom. 3:5). Praise be to God that the confession made to the Father on my behalf or on behalf of any of my loved ones will not rely on my memory but on Christ's!

MUTUAL BROTHERLY CONSOLATION AND FORGIVENESS

SCOTT KEITH

As for myself, I judge the loss of all one's possessions easier to bear than the loss of one faithful friend.

—MARTIN LUTHER

Friendship is unnecessary, like philosophy, like art . . . It has no survival value; rather it is one of those things which give value to survival.

—C. S. LEWIS, *THE FOUR LOVES*

In episode twenty-five of the *Thinking Fellows* podcast, Dr. Rosenbladt and I interviewed Pastor Joel Fitzpatrick, one of the hosts of *Front Porch with the Fitzes*, on the topic of masculinity. It was interesting to me how quickly our conversation turned from masculinity to the subject of male friendships. What has become evident to me over the past several years of research is that the two topics of masculinity and male friendships cannot be separated.

The word that typifies my understanding of what makes male friendships so central to the concept of masculinity is *philia*. *Philia* (φιλία) is the Greek word used to describe nonhomosexual, brotherly love. When Lewis defines the word *philia* in *The Four Loves*, he uses the word "friendship." In the ancient world, *philia* was the most praiseworthy of all forms of love. To the ancients, friendship was the cornerstone of the development of virtue. In the *Nicomachean Ethics*, Aristotle defines *philia* as the reciprocal benevolence that is characteristic only among actual friends, adding, "Without friends, no one would want to live, even if he had all other goods."

Though it is unpopular to say within our modern parlance, the reality is that men need other men with whom they develop strong and loving friendships. They need *philia* love from other men. To be married is wonderful and a blessing, but to be loved by a true friend is sublime. Why? Because it is among the conversation and mutual consolation of brethren that we all—especially men—encounter in a substantially real, physical, and even heartfelt way the proclamation of forgiveness in Christ.

Among Lutherans it is worth noting that even our confessions acknowledge this reality. In what is called Luther's theological last will and testament, the *Smalcald Articles, Part III, Article IV*, he says:

> We will now return to the Gospel, which not merely in one way gives us counsel and aid against sin; for God is superabundantly rich [and liberal] in His grace [and goodness]. First, through the spoken Word by which the forgiveness of sins is preached [He commands to be preached] in the whole world; which is the peculiar office of the Gospel. Secondly, through Baptism. Thirdly, through the holy Sacrament of the Altar. Fourthly, through the power of the keys, and also through the mutual conversation and consolation of brethren, (Matt. 18:20) Where two or three are gathered together, etc.

So then, God's grace comes to us through friendship or, as Luther termed it, fellowship. God's grace is revealed through the proclamation of His forgiveness among those who belong to Christ. The declaration of the gospel of Christ and forgiveness among friends are two of the most powerful *means* God uses to keep us all in His grace.

So why is this particularly important among men? If even a portion of what modern social psychology tells us is right, we, as a church, are missing the boat. What some of my research has taught me is that men acutely need two things: (1) to belong and (2) to be appreciated. To belong is to be a part of something bigger than yourself. For many men in the past, this place to belong was often their church. But the sad fact is that churches today are full of women and lack men. Men do not feel that they belong in church. This lack of belonging inevitably leads to a lack of appreciation. Their absence means that their contribution is neither needed nor appreciated. It is that place where men should feel as though they are needed and belong that has been feminized and turned into something completely unfamiliar and unwelcome.

It is at this point, at the apex of abandonment, where a group of friends will fill in the spiritual and emotional potholes left by our current culture—a culture that is at war with real men and a church that seems to have forgotten all about them—and provide what these appear unwilling to provide: real conversation, real consolation, real forgiveness, real proclamation, real law, and real gospel. Therefore, friendship, especially male friendship, is utterly important. Further, this conversation always enters into real discussions of masculinity because, in my experience, it is only masculine men who recognize what has been lost in our overly feminized world and what is to gain by having real friends with whom one shares a sense of *philia*. Yet these men are rare, for as Lewis says, few value true friendship because so few really experience it.

It is interesting to note that the great reformer Martin Luther seems to have understood this well. Luther had many friends whom he valued highly. While lecturing on John 15:9, Luther reminds his students that we should not easily let go of a real friendship. Luther says:

> Although we are moved to suspicion and displeasure, we should beat these back and remember not to allow them to sever the bond of love and extinguish its fire; but we should cling firmly to our friendship in the face of them . . . This is the joy of the devil, who strives for nothing else but to disturb the love among friends. (Luther, What Luther Says)

Additionally, as Luther was lecturing regarding the split between Abraham and Lot (Gen. 13:5–7), he took the opportunity to give a soliloquy on the spiritual strength and necessity of true friendship.

> Throughout life, a faithful friend is a great blessing (bonum) and a very precious treasure. This is true not only in view of the ordinary dangerous difficulties in which he can offer help and consolation but also in view of spiritual temptations. For even though your heart is thoroughly confirmed by the Holy Spirit, there is nonetheless a great advantage in having a friend whom you can talk about religion and from whom you may hear words of comfort. (Luther, What Luther Says)

Lewis may be right; friendship may not be necessary (though I believe he thought that friendship was very necessary), but I have come to believe that mutual brotherly consolation and forgiveness are. These have more "survival value" than I can describe within the confines of this limited format. Brotherly consolation and forgiveness are life and death, and I would, like Luther, sooner lose everything I own than lose the mutual conversation and consolation of my male brethren, my friends. Praise be to God for forgiveness among friends!

THE REBELLION
OF FRIENDSHIP

PAUL KOCH

At Scott Keith's Ph.D. celebration party, after locating the bottle of rye and settling into a few conversations with old acquaintances, Scott was escorted to a chair in the middle of the room so his friends might offer a toast and even share an embarrassing memory or two with the group. When I was asked to share a few words, I also told stories of our long journey of friendship (marked most notably by the quest for booze and coffee at proper intervals), but it was obvious that it was far more difficult to speak directly about friendship.

I suppose this has always been the case. In his lengthy discourse on friendship, Cicero certainly gives us delightful quotes such as: "Great and numerous as are the blessings of friendship, this certainly is the sovereign one, that it gives us bright hopes for the future and forbids weakness and despair." Yet there is so much that is left unsaid in his work and so much that goes unexamined in our understanding of friendship.

C. S. Lewis takes on the topic of friendship in his work *The Four Loves*. He is just as quotable, but he seems to recognize the limits to which one can speak about friendship. He observes, "Lovers are always talking to one another about their love; friends hardly ever about their Friendship. Lovers are normally face-to-face, absorbed in each other; friends, side by side, absorbed in some common interest." So I could talk about hiking through the snow in Fort Wayne with Scott to get a bottle of booze but not so much about the quality of our friendship. That is simply something friends don't speak much about.

I don't bring this up to try to take the works of Cicero or Lewis and somehow carry them forward. Rather, it's because our culture's recent silence on the topic of friendship seems to be the dreaded calm before the storm. We are in danger of losing something significant if we lose the powerful force of friendship.

We don't talk seriously about friendship anymore. We don't endeavor to figure out what makes it work. And even worse, we might not even know what friendship really is. We have lots of so-called friends. We have "friends" on Facebook, "friends" in the office, and "friends" from school. These "friends" are easily made and quickly forgotten. "Friend" is the title we give acquaintances, but real friendship is in short supply. When we lose friendship, we lose the great corrective to the masses, the resistance to the common pull of our culture, and the heartbeat of rebellion.

To quote Lewis again, "If our master, by force or by propaganda about 'Togetherness' or by unobtrusively making privacy and unplanned leisure impossible, even succeed in producing a world where all are Companions and none are Friends, they will have removed certain dangers, and will also have taken from us that is almost our strongest safeguard against complete servitude" (Lewis, *The Four Loves*). At its core, friendship is a rebellion. True, it can be in service of both virtue and vice. It can seek to elevate the mind, pollute the liver, or both at the same time. But without it, we will be overcome by the current.

My point is that to make a stand in the world, to resist the status quo, friendship is necessary. We don't have to fully understand the nature of friendship or examine it like Cicero or Lewis, but we damn well better care. Hold fast to your friends. Don't allow this force to be so easily dispersed by a society that values the brevity of a conversation in 140 characters. Friends standing side by side will still do what others deem impossible. Let the rebellion begin!

THE JOY OF SEX AND CHURCH

PAUL KOCH

Eighteen years after my bride walked down the aisle with me, having just exchanged vows before God and a whole congregation of witnesses, I was boiling water for coffee because we were camping with the kids. We ate a relaxed breakfast cooked by my wife and began to break camp and load up the minivan. After eighteen years of marriage, we piled all five of our kids and our dog into the car to make the trip down the mountain. I leaned over, kissed my bride, and said, "Happy Anniversary!" As I drove, I began to wonder how we ended up here. Did we envision this eighteen years ago? Did we plan for this?

Now, when I wonder about this, I don't just mean the kids (whom I love) or the minivan (which I hate). Rather, I mean this incredible life that we have together. Did we envision a life in which strength, support, encouragement, correction, forgiveness, desire, and satisfaction would be found in each other? Did I plan for a life in which my bride's presence alone would give the courage to engage in my calling with the boldness and recklessness required to do it well?

Perhaps it was included in the statement of intent I spoke on my wedding day:

Will you have this woman to be your wedded wife, to live together in the holy estate of matrimony as God ordained it? Will you nourish and cherish her as Christ loved His body, the Church, giving Himself up for her? Will you love, honor, and keep her in sickness and in health and, forsaking all others, remain united to her alone, so long as you both shall live? Then say: I will.

But to be honest, though I know I did, I don't remember saying those words. I don't think I planned for much of anything beyond embracing the woman standing before me. I don't know what I envisioned we would be doing eighteen years later, though I'm sure I hoped sex would still be a major part of the routine.

How did we end up here? How did I go from an instinctual desire to protect and care for this woman, a desire fueled by erotic love and the joy of sex, to a life in which we walk side by side in a deep bond of friendship? How is it that we didn't become the stereotype of the modern marriage, which views itself as a form of imprisonment rather than freedom? While it is not all sunshine and rainbows, this life together is one I would never exchange for something else.

As far as I can tell, the answer has to do with church—precisely the gifts of Christ, which call, gather, and enlighten the children of God.

You see, unbeknown to us, these gifts did something to our love for each other. They did something to our life that was beyond what we had planned or imagined. Now, you might guess that it somehow strengthened what we already had. Somehow, going to church made marriage that much better because it provided something that was lacking. And it is certainly true that the proclamation of law and gospel to a husband and wife, to mothers, fathers, and their children, provides strength and endurance that this world cannot offer on its own. But it's not just that church helped us get through tough times. No, the gifts of Christ changed the very structure of our relationship.

The gifts of Christ turned us from facing toward one another to walking beside each other.

Because of church, because of the impact of a word outside of ourselves, we grew into a habit of conversation and consolation in our relationship. When God's law and His gospel invaded our life over and again, we were left to make confession, repent, wonder, and question. Time and again, we found that His gifts called us into a life where we lived along a common endeavor instead of just satisfying our own needs. The gifts found at church freed us to care for one another in radical ways we never planned for or imagined. They called us to both ask for and speak the language of forgiveness.

Eighteen years later, we find that we've been on an incredible journey shaped by the blessings of our Lord. And through it all, through the ups and the down, the tears and the laughter, there has been an insane amount of joy—in sex, adventure, children, questioning, confession, absolution, dreams, and surprises. For the joy of Christ's gifts have turned my wife and lover into my friend and companion along the way.

WELCOME TO THE REBELLION

PAUL KOCH

Hence if our masters, by force or by propaganda about "Togetherness" or by unobtrusively making privacy and unplanned leisure impossible, ever succeed in producing a world where all are Companions and none are Friends, they will have removed certain dangers, and will also have taken from us what is almost our strongest safeguard against complete servitude.

—C. S. LEWIS, *THE FOUR LOVES*

At its core, friendship is a rebellion.

I've done a lot of thinking about *The Jagged Word*—what we're trying to do, how we started, and where we're going. To be honest, it's not always easy to explain what we're doing or where we're going. The explanations seem to be somewhat fluid. These days, I imagine that different authors on *The Jagged Word* would explain it differently. Our agenda here (if you can call it that) doesn't exactly promote a unified vision. The agenda is to give the authors the freedom to write—the freedom to inspire and enrage, to be boring and aimless. They are free to find their own voices in the shifting mess that is church and world. The unifying core that gives shape to it all is the powerful and unpredictable thing we call friendship.

Week in and week out, the production of *The Jagged Word* is the result of friendship. All the writers are people whom I trust, but I've also sat with them in bars into the early morning hours. Together, we've argued about theology and life, laughed out loud, confessed, and worshiped. *The Jagged Word* doesn't have a governing board, mission statement, or strategic growth plan. Instead, we have the unpredictable victories and failures that flow from friendship.

It turns out that wondering how we started is the key to understanding where we are going and what we are trying to accomplish. I'm privileged to be able to call these authors my friends. In fact, I believe friendship is a rare and valuable commodity. Most of us have very few true friends whom we can trust when the shit hits the fan and we need a shoulder to cry on or a hand to pass us a drink. Friends are not "yes men." They are not people with whom you must always agree. A friend may be an inspirational example, role model, or cheerleader. Then again, he may be a drunkard or a heretic, but a friend won't abandon you, no matter where you fall on the spectrum.

By nature, friendship is not easily controlled by outside forces seeking to bring order and uniformity. At its core, friendship has a spirit of rebellion against those who would control it through shame on the one hand and pride on the other.

Friendship has a nasty habit of continuing when everyone else is screaming for it to stop. It endures even when it doesn't make much sense to do so. Yet what we have found on *The Jagged Word* is that there is a place for this beautiful rebellion in the conversations that matter. In fact, the unpredictability of friendship has found an extension in the readers of our work. Through your comments, likes, and dislikes, whether agreeing or disagreeing, you help shape where this is all going.

The Jagged Word is not the party line. We don't peer review our work or send it through doctrinal review. We submit it just like we would in the back corner of the bar. It can be raw and wrong, or it can be powerful, transformative, and orthodox, but it is never driven by some other directive greater than our friendship—and whatever happens to inspire us or piss us off at that particular moment.

I'm proud of what this site has become, and I honestly have no idea where it will go. I am overjoyed that you've joined the rebellion. But truth be told, even if you didn't join us, I doubt we would stop. Such is friendship.

I AM
FRODO BAGGINS

SCOTT KEITH

did not immediately love J. R. R. Tolkien's *The Hobbit* or *The Lord of the Rings* trilogy. I was a latecomer to reading them, and I initially found them slow and hard to finish. After all, "and they were walking, and walking, and walking, and then they walked some more." But over time and with some help from friends, I have come to love these works and what they represent. Since then, I have read the books several times, listened to them as audiobooks (my wife's reaction to the voice of Gollum at 1:00 a.m. on Highway 395 in the middle of nowhere in Nevada was not great), and watched all the movies several times.

If you are less familiar with these works of Tolkien, the story lines follow the adventures of two hobbits, small and kindly humanoids, who acquire and then attempt to destroy the "One Ring," which is the most powerful ring of the Rings of Power. The older of the two hobbits, Bilbo Baggins, who is one of the main characters in *The Hobbit*, is responsible for acquiring—really stealing—the ring. The younger of the two, Frodo Baggins, who is one of the main characters in *The Lord of the Rings*, is tasked with destroying the ring. As it turns out, the One Ring is evil and links the ring bearer in a very personal way to the personification of all evil, Sauron.

As each of the stories progress, other plotlines are revealed, friendships are forged and lost, adventures are had, magic is revealed, and common life full of ale drinking, eating, traveling, and pipe smoking is lived. What is not to love, right? In *The Lord of the Rings* trilogy, it is Frodo who reluctantly accepts the task—vocation, really—of destroying the One Ring. This can only happen if he takes the ring to where it was forged and throws it into the fires of Mount Doom. What Frodo discovers is that the evil and the power of the One Ring are very difficult to bear and to resist.

Time and time again, Frodo seems to want to do the right thing, and on occasion, he does it. After all, he agrees to take the ring on this perilous journey full of hardships to destroy it. When he exclaims, "I will take the ring to Mordor," he agrees to persevere, run the race, and see this thing through to the end. But he is no real hero along the way. On more than one occasion, he succumbs to the ring's temptation, as his Uncle Bilbo had as well. In the process, he receives a wound that never really heals and plagues him throughout the story.

In fact, there are times when it seems that the ring is too heavy for him to bear. On more than one occasion, I was sure that he would not make it one more step, let alone all the way to Mount Doom. He is partnered along the way with another hobbit, Samwise Gamgee. Sam is Frodo's loyal companion and friend. But the deeper into their journey the two travel, the more Frodo is influenced by the ring's power and evil. Though Frodo remains capable of wonderful kindness, he is more and more tormented by the One Ring. At one point, he even gives into the temptation of one of his more evil and untrustworthy companions, Gollum, and sends his true and good friend Sam away.

If Frodo is the hero of *The Lord of the Rings*, he is a poor hero. He is reluctant, scared, and at times sickly, weak, and apt to succumb to the temptation of the One Ring. He even turns on his friend and loyal companion. But he is good too. Frodo loves his friend Sam. He is occasionally very brave, and he perseveres, albeit in a very imperfect manner, to the fires of Mount Doom. Even at the end, the battle inside Frodo is evident. Frodo eventually manages to get the ring to the mountain and into the fire, but at a great cost. Just when he has the chance to do the right thing and cast the ring into the fire, he gives in to the temptation of the One Ring one last time. The ring's destruction comes almost despite Frodo's intentions and not because of his heroic virtue. The final moments of the journey end with good being made from evil intentions in an unexpected way.

I say that I am a Frodo because I am no hero, though I am capable of great heroism. I am not good, yet I have manifested wonderful goodness to others. I am weak of spirit, though others often rely on my strength. I am sickly of heart and soul, though I thank God for my health and well-being. I have been a great friend to many, yet I have often neglected my friends and cast them out of my life. If I am the great deliverer, I am also the most destructive person I know. The weight of my sin bears down upon me daily, just as the One Ring seemed so heavy to Frodo as to prevent him from taking even one more step.

Frodo is simultaneously a hero and a wounded agent of the One Ring. I am at one and the same time a saint of God and an evil sinner. I think that Tolkien's brilliance in these tales was not so much in presenting a clear Christ figure, as C. S. Lewis often did, but in presenting clearly human figures in the form of elves, wizards, dwarfs, men, and hobbits. Being a lifelong Roman Catholic, I'm not sure if J. R. R. Tolkien understood *Simul Iustus et Peccator*, but something like it was certainly revealed in the characters he created. This is the theological concept that all the saved, all the saints, are at the same time justified before God by grace—through faith, not by works but because of Christ—and yet remain seen as sinners according to their own works and merit.

In Romans chapter 7, the apostle Paul says, "So I find this law at work: Although I want to do good, evil is right there with me. For in my inner being I delight in God's law; but I see another law at work in me, waging war against the law of my mind and making me a prisoner of the law of sin at work within me. What a wretched man I am! Who will rescue me from this body that is subject to death? Thanks be to God, who delivers me through Jesus Christ our Lord!"

Our reliance is not in our own, even our renewed, good natures. Even when we want to be the hero of the story, we find that there is evil with us. Yet ours is not a fabricated tale that only points to the truth in a clouded way. Our story is the true story of hope, grace, victory, and freedom. Our hero is the Christ, who has saved us from sin, death, and the power of the devil. He has won the battle and cast evil into the fire, and he will not let us down. Even while we were yet sinners, and though we remain sinners, He has delivered and will deliver us from this body of death.

So though I am weak like Frodo and no real hero at all, though I sin daily and do not deserve His deliverance, though I am just a saved sinner, Christ died and rose for me! I have only one hope and that is in Jesus Christ. Thus I say with Paul, "Who will rescue me from this body that is subject to death? Thanks be to God, who delivers me through Jesus Christ our Lord!" (Rom. 7:24–25). Paul also says, "And to the one who does not work but believes in him who justifies the ungodly, his faith is counted as righteousness . . ." (Rom. 4:5).

FRIENDSHIP

FROM PISS TROUGH
TO HORSE TROUGH

SCOTT KEITH

Because our expression is imperfect we need friendship to fill up
the imperfections.
—G. K. CHESTERTON, *ILLUSTRATED LONDON NEWS*, JUNE 6, 1931

R ecent events in the world of evangelical Christianity
have illustrated what I already knew: men need more
real friends. It seems that men don't have real friends at
all. I think that people who don't know me well would say of me
that I don't have many friends, comparing me to their perception
of other people. Maybe they would be right, but I think that I
have more true friends than most. What is not in great supply in
my life are loads upon loads of those whom most call "friends." I
merely call them acquaintances. This can get confusing. For what
is a friend if not an acquaintance one sees often? I don't think
that's true. While it may be true that proximity and frequency are
usually a part of the friendship equation, these things alone do
not make friendship. A friend is someone who is present from
the piss trough to the horse trough and back again. Friends stand

together through the embarrassing exposure, into brokenness, and are on the other side when forgiveness is granted and brotherhood regained.

If you are a man around my same age or older, you probably have memories of peeing alongside other men and boys in what can only be described as a trough. For me, this was most often at my little parochial school, Grace Lutheran School in Lancaster, California. In the men's bathroom, next to the seventh and eighth grade room was what can only be described as a trough for boys to piss in. We could line a dozen boys up at that trough, no waiting in line, no halt of the story or conversation, just peeing and talking.

To women, I'm sure this seems somewhat outrageous. Yet at that trough we learned a lot about one another (beyond the vulgar and obvious). The thing is, at least while I was in school, there was nothing weird about it. I was almost always next to my best friends while pissing at that trough. The conversation that began on the playground never needed to stop just because someone needed to pee. The trough provided camaraderie and an open forum. You'd be amazed at how free one can feel when everyone is exposed—all pretense disappears.

The first part of friendship is exposure. There is a bare and gritty honesty needed between true friends. These friends are not the people that we "poke" or label as "friends" on Facebook. These are the people who truly know who we are. Our friends know who we are because we have either been laid bare or laid ourselves bare in front of them. When we sin, it is no surprise to them because they know us to be a sinner. After all, we have stood shoulder to shoulder at the piss trough. They know when we need a trip to the horse trough.

There is a scene in the movie *Wyatt Earp* starring Kevin Costner in which Doc Holiday fights with his girlfriend Big Nose Kate. Kate is a prostitute; Doc is an alcoholic as well as a renowned killer, and the two are about to murder one another. Doc is drunk as usual and is absolutely out of control. I have heard that we are all only three missteps away from losing control of everything.

If that is true, in the scene Doc is presented as if he had already taken about two and a half steps. Just then, his friend Wyatt Earp busts into the room and breaks up the fight.

Wyatt breaking up the fight is not important here. Rather, it is when Wyatt takes Doc downstairs and repeatedly dunks his head in a horse trough until Doc "comes to his senses." It is at this point that Wyatt asks Doc, "What's wrong with you Doc?" Doc's reply is honesty born of being exposed to and by his friend. Doc explains, "I am dying of tuberculosis. Everyone who knows me hates me. I sleep with the nastiest whore in Kansas, and every morning I wake up surprised that I have to spend another day in the piss-hole world." Wyatt's response makes the whole movie for me when he says, "Not everybody that knows you hates you, Doc." Doc then looks up at Wyatt, and if you watch carefully, you might discern that at that very moment the world is no longer a "piss hole" to Doc. Individually considered, there are not many important words in the sentence Wyatt proclaims to Doc. But strung together, Wyatt's words become a proclamation of forgiveness, friendship, and finally brotherhood. Thus Wyatt's forgiveness changes Doc's world.

Friendship is exposure, brokenness, forgiveness, and brotherhood. We like to envision law and gospel as sets of complicated and systematized definitions that we willfully recognize, discern, and apply. Yet I often think that God didn't intend law and gospel to work that way. Law and gospel play out in the everyday lives of our relationships, and if we have actual friends, they are especially present. To our friends we are exposed, laid bare with our heads dunked in the horse trough of the law, only to be forgiven while sitting in the mud next to that same trough. Both the law and the gospel come to us on the lips of others, sometimes even through our friends. The law drowns us, and then we are made children and brothers again by the simple—yet not simplistic—proclamation of the gospel. Thus if we have good friends, we often find ourselves living life from the piss trough to the horse trough. My prayer is that friendship not be a rare commodity to you.

SIMPLE PLEASURES,
∧ BROTHERHOOD,
AND CALM DELIGHT

PART FIVE
GOOD SMOKE, GOOD DRINK, AND GOOD FELLOWSHIP

HOW THE CIGAR ∧
CAN SAVE AMERICA

THE ARGUMENT ∧
AGAINST PIPE SMOKING

∧
PINING FOR GRANDPA

∧ MANHATTANS,
DECORATIVE SWORDS,
AND A MACK TRUCK ASHTRAY

SIMPLE PLEASURES, BROTHERHOOD, AND CALM DELIGHT

SCOTT KEITH

Give a man a pipe he can smoke,
Give a man a book he can read,
And his home is bright with calm delight,
Though the room be poor indeed.

—ALFRED DUNHILL, 1924

In Christmas of 2014, I got a new pipe, as did my two sons. I started smoking pipes while I was in college. I have thus smoked a pipe off and on (mostly off while my children were younger) for the last twenty years or so. There is something to smoking a pipe that changes the way I think. It takes patience to smoke a pipe, and I am not a patient person. When I smoke a pipe, I am forced to slow down and take the time necessary to tend to the little embers that I took such care creating in the first place. If I move too fast or ignore my charge, the embers will extinguish, and I will need to relight and start the tending process again.

Smoking a pipe takes time. While I smoke my pipe, I can give myself a wonderful gift—the time to do those things that I do not do in the hustle and bustle of my normally hectic day. While smoking a pipe, I will often read a book. While tending my embers, I regularly contemplate God's glorious creation and my place in it. Better yet, I often smoke my pipe in the company of others. Sometimes I am with students or alumni from the university. Often, I am with my friend Paul Koch. But most often, I am with my sons Caleb and Joshua. The simple pleasure of smoking a pipe with my students, friends, or sons provides us the time to talk with one another, banter, admire one another's pipes, and, better yet, enjoy the brotherhood of other men.

I find a deep rejuvenation falls upon me during these times when I allow myself to enjoy the simple pleasures of my pipe and the brotherhood of other men. I don't know if Luther smoked a pipe or not, but I know that he felt the rejuvenation that comes from the fellowship of brothers in the faith around a table over-flowing with the simple pleasures of Katherine's home-brewed bier. In fact, he wrote about such times being nearly sacramen-tal in the *Smalcald Articles*. There, Luther confesses that the gos-pel gives consolation and bestows grace. His argument is that these gifts are bestowed through preaching the gospel, baptism, the Lord's Supper, confession and absolution, and "through the mutual conversation and consolation of brethren 'where two or three are gathered in my name' (Matt. 18:20)." What else is the mutual consolation and conversation of brethren than joining together in simple pleasures and deep conversation with faithful brothers?

I need time to slow down and smoke my pipe. I need time to enjoy that good book that has taken up residence on my night-stand, collecting dust rather than imparting knowledge and wis-dom. In our intensely paced world, I need to slow down and do something that takes time and careful tending, simply for the pure enjoyment of doing that thing. I need to enjoy simple pleasures and great conversations with friends and the camaraderie that comes with those endeavors. You may find that you need these things as well. If you do, remember the words of Luther and Alfred Dunhill. The gospel is handed over in the mutual consolation and conversation of brethren, and a man with a pipe brings a calm delight to his home. My advice to you is to enjoy the simple pleasures of life, the brotherhood of faithful friends, and the calm delight that comes from smoking your pipe.

Quite Kindly,
The (today) Not-So Cantankerous Critic (Pappy)

HOW THE CIGAR CAN SAVE AMERICA

GRAHAM GLOVER

There is only one solution remaining. All others have failed. Democratic liberalism? No, thank you. Republican conservatism? Not a chance. Green Party environmentalism? Uh, no. Libertarianism of any kind? Never. Never. Never. My fellow Americans, we are down to our final hope. To save America, our country must embrace the cigar. I implore you to heed my call. The cigar's time is now.

You think I'm kidding? You don't know me very well. What's so great about the cigar? Everything. Absolutely everything. You must understand, I'm not talking about Swisher Sweets here. I'm referring to a beautifully handcrafted Dominican, Honduran, or Nicaraguan cigar. I'm dead serious; more Americans need to learn the art of smoking a cigar.

Why? Quite simply, smoking a cigar takes time. A good cigar takes forty-five to ninety minutes to smoke. It's forty-five to ninety minutes of pure joy. And to fix our country, we need this time with one another. We need to relearn the art of enjoying one another's company. We need to relax a lot more than most of us do. And in smoking cigars, I'm convinced we can finally figure out how to move forward as a country together and not as a divided lot.

Some of my best counseling sessions with soldiers take place over cigars. We aren't rushed to go anywhere. We are typically outside, which means we aren't distracted by computers or people knocking on the door. We even seem to ignore our cell phones when they ring during this time. Everything else seems to stop during this "sacred" time of cigar smoking. In addition to enjoying the taste of whatever stick we are smoking, we always seem to make progress on the issue that brought us together. I think this happens because the act of smoking a cigar allows us to relax and focus. Additionally, I usually befriend those whom I have a cigar with, and our time together almost always extends beyond what we planned.

And it is here, in the act of engaging in meaningful and sincere conversation, that I learn about soldiers, myself, and how we can serve one another and the army.

So here's my suggestion for our policy makers: sit down regularly throughout the week, preferably with someone on the other side of the aisle, and have a cigar. Talk honestly and earnestly about where you differ. Talk, then listen. Talk and listen some more. If you disagree, that's fine. Relax, light up another cigar, and go at it some more. I don't know how you will find a solution, but you will. The cigar will help. If you can't agree on policy, agree on the wonder of the cigar you are smoking. It's a start, and it will work. Trust me. Trust the cigar.

Above all, I implore all of you to find time to engage others in meaningful conversation. We moderns have lost the art of conversing. And without regular dialogue with those closest to us, especially our adversaries, our democracy and way of life will not endure. This is one of the reasons I love cigars. Like most of us, I am pulled in countless directions throughout the day. The demands of my job and my family consume most every waking hour of my day. But none of us are *that* busy. None of us are *that* important. And all of us can find a few hours during the week to stop what we are doing, sit down, light up a cigar, relax, focus, and talk.

The cigar's time is now. It can save us. Oh yes, it can.

THE ARGUMENT AGAINST PIPE SMOKING

AN ETHICAL QUIDDITY

SCOTT KEITH

A TRIBUTE TO ROBERT FARRAR CAPON*

The president *pro tempore* of the United States Senate was attempting to call the senators to order. The senators—chief deliberators of that hallowed and august body—were busy milling around the floor. Twice, he sounded his gavel, punctuating his intention. Clearing his throat, he announced the bill then under consideration, a national act intended to ban the smoking of pipes from both indoor and outdoor public spaces.

Turning, he then recognized the distinguished senator from California—the very woman who had sponsored the bill. She rose to address the Senate. "Thank you, Mr. President. Distinguished

---

* Robert Farrar Capon was an Episcopal priest, theologian, and author. He was also a food critic for the *New York Times*. This piece is inspired by his article "The Case against Heavy Cream: A Metaphysical Quibble," which first appeared in the October 5, 1983, edition of the *New York Times*.

colleagues and my fellow Americans, we have quibbled over this legislation long enough; I move that we submit this bill to a vote."

Suddenly, the senior senator from Texas interrupted, "Now just hold on here one gosh darn minute." His rich and sonorous drawl hung heavy in the air. "I want to hear the bill one last time before we make this here thing final." At this request, a clerk near the rostrum rose and began to read the bill aloud to the gathered senators.

The clerk intoned, "Whereas overwhelming consensus suggests that exposure to tobacco smoke (whether directly or by the inhalation of incidental second-hand smoke) is known to be dangerous and cancer-causing; and whereas there is no discernible public benefit known to accrue from pipe smoking; and whereas pipe smoking can thereby be considered pointless and accordingly concluded to be a wholly useless endeavor that subverts the safety of society and the public good."

The clerk concluded, "Therefore, be it resolved that the smoking of tobacco pipes in any and all public venues both indoors and out of doors be completely banned; resolved further that this prohibition will include restaurants and restaurant patios, tobacco shops, parks, sporting venues, as well as bars and bar patios; resolved finally that this act prohibit the smoking of pipes in any private home located within 5,000 feet from any school, so as not to tempt the children who might see someone smoking their pipe or catch a whiff of their pungent smoke as it rises into what is commonly known to be the public air, which we all use for respiration."

Satisfied at this, the senator from California rose from her seat to exclaim, "Over the course of our debate regarding this public health and morality bill, we have heard both from advocates and from detractors, and we have availed ourselves of all of the latest research concerning pipe smoking and its deleterious personal—as well as public—health dangers." She then sighed heavily as she elaborated upon their deliberations. "It is a shame that during the course of our research we were forced to smell pipe smoke as we ventured into those smoking clubs and backwoods bars that still allow these atrocities to continue. I still can't get the smell of the Virginia Blend out of my hair."

At this, the senator from Texas, sensing that he was losing the argument, interjected, "Madam Senator, we concede that most studies show that pipe smoking presents a moderate risk of an increased propensity toward various cancers. We also concede that second-hand smoke has, in some studies, been shown to have some unhealthy effects."

Hearing the Texan's concessions, the Californian puffed up, believing that she had won the day. The senator from Texas furrowed his brow, raised his shaming finger, and continued, "These increases and these effects are either moderate or negligible."

The senator from California wheeled her gaze back to the senator from Texas, agape with shock as he continued: "Surely, we all agree—including yourself, Madam Senator—that sucking on a tailpipe is hazardous to the health. Moderate pipe smoking is no more harmful than getting stuck in traffic and breathing the inevitable car exhaust fumes while one waits on the highway, and we might agree, a good deal more healthful."

He was beaming as she shrunk back in her chair. "But both pipe smoking and car exhaust present some health concerns. The logic of your bill, Madam Senator, suggests that we manage the risk and temper the hazard by prohibition—that we ban both in the interest of public safety. Ought we to ban driving as well?"

"Also," he said in his most Texas twang, "Is there no data to suggest smoking a pipe—moderately of course—might actually be *beneficial* to one's health?"

Now the entire Senate was in an uproar; some cheered, and others jeered. A few well-placed bangs of the gavel by the president *pro tempore* and the room came back to order.

With control regained, the senator from Texas continued, "When I gather with my friends to smoke my pipe at our little watering hole around the corner from my house, a couple of distinctly 'healthy' things happen to me."

A quiet calm and look of peaceful nostalgia seemed to set-tle on his face. "First, I slow down. Smoking and caring for the embers in a pipe take time—a welcome respite in a frantic world. Second, I talk to my pals. I get to experience truly the peace that can only be had by spending good times in leisurely conversa-tion. Finally, I think about things I wouldn't otherwise have a chance to contemplate—things like right and wrong, good and bad, holy and depraved. In short, I get to be human."

The senator's robust and aromatic words wafted and wisped around the room. The normally raucous Senate floor assumed the feel of a rustic country lodge, as if an old man were sitting before a fireplace telling his family about growing up in the good old days—the halcyon days when men could be men. He had the floor now; no one would dare take it from him.

He calmly explained the importance of being human. "You see, the smoke don't matter. Your comfort and my comfort don't matter. All that matters is freedom. To be human is to desire to be free."

The entire Senate looked in amazement at the passion on the senator's face as he said, "It seems to me that the point isn't just to live and be 'safe.' And so, we don't need this bill. Maybe what we need is a little more friendship, a little more time to relax, a little more smoke to calm the nerves and enrich the conversation."

He leveled his gaze sternly into the eyes of the senator from California and said, "And to say that pipe smoking is pointless is utter nonsense. Nothing of such utility can be pointless! If pipe smoking is pointless, hell, nothing has meaning then. Wine is pointless. Your Diet Coke, Madam Senator, is pointless. We are pointless, and this Senate is then pointless. Why heck, the whole dang world is pointless from that point of view."

His final remarks set many back on their heels. "Pipe smok-ing is good! Pipe smoking is not only good; it's sublime. It's good for me, and it's good for our society. It shows that we embrace freedom, love quality, enjoy friendship, value time to think, and attempt to answer the bigger questions in life. In short, the only ethical choice for us is to send this bill back from whence it came—the gates of hell."

Well, we all know how the vote would have gone if this story were true. The next time you enjoy some well-earned camaraderie with your friends, attempt to light up your finely crafted smoking implement on the patio of your favorite bar, and are asked—politely or not—to put it out for the sake of others, think of this story.

Do we as a society desire to be safe or to be free? Do we want to be a society that strives for value, quality, truth, and beauty, or are we to forever be content with being protected from ourselves? Probing the meaningful questions of life takes time and discourse with friends. For many of us, this is one of the foremost reasons that we love smoking our pipes as much as we do. This type of companionship moves past camaraderie into the realm of brotherhood. Nowhere in the whole of God's creation will such brotherly love and assurance be practiced as amid those who recline together in discussion smoking their pipes. The desire to sit around a public table with friends and a pipe is not merely natural; it's primeval.

The ethics of pipe smoking, if such an animal might exist, extend far beyond questions of safety and comfort. Pipe smoking goes right to the heart of the contemplation of meaning. To some, smoking may be unnecessary, but our eyes are often opened to many good and true things by means of seemingly inessential things. Seen through this lens, what could be more necessary than smoking a pipe?

The only ethical choice may be to embrace freedom, love quality, enjoy friendship, value time to think, and attempt to answer the bigger questions in life. And these would be facilitated by friends at our side and a pipe in our hand. As Edward George Bulwer-Lytton, a nineteenth-century English novelist and poet, wrote, "A pipe is the fountain of contemplation, the source of pleasure, the companion of the wise; and the man who smokes thinks like a philosopher and acts like a Samaritan."

As for me, I'm going to head to the patio of my favorite watering hole, light my pipe, and wait around to see who kicks me out first for the sake of perceived necessity. Who knows? Maybe some friends will join me.

Happy Smoking!

PINING FOR GRANDPA

SCOTT KEITH

When I took my children to see the new Marvel Comics movie *Dr. Strange*, I was more struck by the young man sitting in front of me than I was by the movie. He was what I would call a hipster. He wore hiking boots with rolled-up jeans, a buttoned-up wool flannel shirt, and a beanie positioned above his ears with the pointy top rising off the top of his head. Frankly, he looked like a skinny lumberjack parading through the streets of San Juan Capistrano.

Now, before I get too critical of his attire, it should be noted that I was wearing boots, jeans, a wool flannel shirt, and a canvas cap. The only qualitative differences are that I am not skinny and I have a beard to complete the San Juan lumberjack look. In my defense, I could say that I have lived in the mountains most of my adult life and that the beard-and-flannel look is nothing new for me. In fact, the "mountain man" look has been a part of my regular repertoire since my teens. But this does not change the fact that both the young hipster and I are pining to be like our grandpas (in his case, maybe his great-grandpa).

What does this mean? Well, I believe that some modern men long to be like men of the past. Those men possessed a character or quality that we greatly desire to acquire ourselves. What is that quality? Masculinity.

As I ponder the root and effect of this reality, I'm burdened by the actuality that my boys have grown up in a world where what was once a given is now an open question, even among a group of manly men. My friend Adam Francisco is a navy vet (the real deal). Overall, he's a very manly man. He shoots, hunts, fishes, fixes stuff, works hard, and, in general, handles his shit. As he and I frequently discuss this topic over booze and smoke, we are often stumped to put our fingers on just what is missing. Most often, we resort to examples from history or our own pasts, hence pining for Grandpa.

By all accounts, my grandpa was a badass. He was a World War II vet who served in the European theater. He, like many vets, brought home war booty. His was an authentic German Luger, which he was reported to have taken off a dead German soldier whom he killed. That's hard core by any reckoning. While I was growing up, he worked as an aviation mechanic for Lockheed Martin Skunk Works in Palmdale, California, where he wrenched on aircraft like the U2, the SR71, and other kick-ass planes. He could fix anything, build anything, and fight anything. To me, he was indestructible. He daily wore a flannel shirt and a blue beanie, which was perched above his ears just like the young man in the movie theater. For a time, I took to wearing my beanie just like his. I was pining after Grandpa.

Why? Well, it's simple. I wanted to be like my grandpa, and I still do. I want to be capable, strong, and courageous. I want to handle my shit and take care of my family. Our society has declared that there is no discernable difference between men and women, and yet every cell in my body tells me that this is just not the case. When I remember my grandpa, my mind rarely conjures the same qualities that I would attribute to my grandmother. I think this is an important reality that the modern-day lumberjack hipster understands better than most.

I think it's all too easy to disparage the hipster of our day. Those young adults who seem at times all too put together, all too interested in handmade quality, and all too focused on nostalgia are easy to criticize. But maybe we ought to recognize that these young men are on the run. Many of them are running from an ideology that has taught them that it is beneath them to demarcate themselves as men, to learn to fix anything, build anything, and fight anything—to be a man pining after the qualities of Grandpa.

I see some of their attempts as tragically misplaced and overdone. However, I often see the desire in their eyes to be more than they currently are. I see that many of these young men feel out of place in our overly feminized culture and that they want to cry out and, in fact, are crying out through the way the dress and their attempts to live lives of quality. I see that they desire a time and a set of rituals that honor them for being manly men, and I think they need a group of men around them that will teach them just what that means.

Paul Koch and I have discussed this topic at length, and I addressed it, at least in part, in my book *Being Dad: Father as a Picture of God's Grace*. In fact, I lecture quite a bit on the subject when I'm out and about promoting the book. Every time I do, I am inevitably asked these simple questions by older men: "What can we do about it? How can we help?" Most often I say that I don't have any clear answers. But recently, after teaching *Being Dad* at Grace Lutheran Church in Ventura, Paul asked me that same question again, and now my friend is taking a stab at finding an answer.

Paul meets with a group of men on the first Tuesday of every month at 7:00 p.m. at Dexter's Camera shop in downtown Ventura to talk and, I would guess, to pine after Grandpa. In years gone by, such meetings may not have been necessary (though I think that the past prevalence of men's clubs and lodges argue otherwise), but now I believe they are. Men need to know that it is OK to be men—to desire the traits of men from days gone by.

Being a man is all about being capable, strong, courageous, and gracious. If the young, or the not so young, want to show that by dressing in a way that pines for Grandpa, I say go for it. As for me, I'll continue to not only miss but also pine for my grandpa every day. See you soon, Grandpa.

MANHATTANS, DECORATIVE SWORDS, AND A MACK TRUCK ASHTRAY

ROSS ENGEL

About a week and a half before Thanksgiving of 2015, my grandma passed away. She had been preceded in death by my grandpa ten years before. She was the last grandparent on my side of the family, and now her house stands empty. Well, it's not quite empty.

Within the walls of Grandma's house are eighty-five years' worth of memories. Inside, there is everything from old books (some dating back to the 1800s), trinkets, jewelry, and souvenirs from trips all over the world, to furniture, photographs, tools, collectibles, and so much more.

At first glance, it is daunting even to consider going through all the things left behind. A dumpster might be the easy answer to eighty-five years' worth of living, traveling, and collecting. However, a careful eye would notice that some of the items are quite valuable. Antiques, china, crystal, artwork, and tools all have potential resale value. But deeper than the potential for financial gain is the simple fact that many of the items in Grandma's house are valuable because of the memories they contain.

My wife and I went with my dad for a quick walk through Grandma's house before we made the drive back home to Florida. In the half hour that we were there, our conversations were filled with storytelling. We shared memories connected with various items. We looked at pictures of family members long deceased. We shared laughter and joy in the midst of sadness and loss as we recalled so many great memories. To me, the things that hold the most value are the things that solicit such strong memories.

The cocktail and rocks glasses reminded me of how my grandparents enjoyed Manhattans when Grandpa got home from work each day. The decorative fencing swords reminded me of how my cousin and I would fence in the basement. Truth be told, we probably weren't supposed to use them to fight, but we had so much fun doing it that Grandpa never got mad. The chrome Mack Truck bull dog ashtray that sat by the door or on Grandpa's desk, which was never used for smoking, held coins and a variety of other items.

There were dozens of items throughout the house that elicited a happy memory or a smile. The sentimental guy in me wants to keep these things, hold them sacred by bringing them home, and display them so that I might always remember the happy times these items represent.

But the reality is, they are just things. Sure, they elicit a memory or two, and that is worth something, but the real treasure that my grandparents left behind was the legacy of their faith. To both of them, it was of great importance to teach their children the faith. They took the time to sing the faith into their children, grandchildren, and great-grandchildren's ears. They embraced the importance of Christian education and encouraged all of us to attend Lutheran schools. They taught that we gather for worship on Sundays so that we might receive our Lord's gifts of forgiveness and life. They taught us the importance of prayer and to confess Jesus with our lips and our lives.

As I helped put together my grandma's funeral, I learned that one of her favorite sections in Scripture is the verses that are traditionally referred to as "the Great Commission":

Go therefore and make disciples of all the nations, baptizing them in the name of the Father and the Son and the Holy Spirit, teaching them to observe all that I commanded you; and lo, I am with you always, even to the end of the age. (Matt. 28:19–20)

Grandma was a Lutheran schoolteacher, the daughter of a Lutheran schoolteacher and principal. For her, it was of the utmost importance that the faith was taught to others. She understood that disciples were created in the waters of Holy Baptism and nurtured through the teaching of God's Holy Word and the receiving of the Lord's Supper. It was important to her that Jesus's commands and words were taught and observed and that we always trust that Jesus keeps His word of promise. He truly is with us until the end of the age.

As those verses were read at my grandma's funeral, I was reminded that the Greek word that Jesus uses in Matthew 28 is sometimes translated as "observe," and other times it is translated as "obey." But the thrust of that verb isn't necessarily obedience or even observance. It carries with it the intention of "holding sacred," or "guarding" and "keeping," the words and commands of Jesus.

We hold so many things sacred within our lives: possessions, treasures, and reputations. We guard them and keep them as though they are of the greatest importance. We fight over these things, snatch them away like looters, and may neglect or destroy to hold onto them. But the reality is, whether those things are the possessions of another, the photographs and memories that we keep, or the things that we've "earned" ourselves, none of them compare with the words of life and salvation that we have in Christ.

His word. His commands. His preaching and teachings. These are the things we should keep, hold sacred, and refuse to let go. For in His word, we find forgiveness, life, and salvation!

As I carefully packed away some of the treasures from my grandma's house, I was reminded of the words of Paul to the church in Philippi. He recounts all the things that he held sacred and dear, all the things he treasured and struggled to hold onto, and realizes their true value. They are nothing when compared to Christ:

> *But whatever things were gain to me, those things I have counted as loss for the sake of Christ. More than that, I count all things to be loss in view of the surpassing value of knowing Christ Jesus my Lord, for whom I have suffered the loss of all things, and count them but rubbish so that I may gain Christ, and may be found in Him, not having a righteousness of my own derived from the Law, but that which is through faith in Christ, the righteousness which comes from God on the basis of faith, that I may know Him and the power of His resurrection and the fellowship of His sufferings, being conformed to His death; in order that I may attain to the resurrection from the dead. (Phil. 4:7–11)*

And all this was written while enjoying a Manhattan and an Oliva Serie V Melanio Maduro cigar, contemplating when it will be appropriate to teach my own young children how to fence with a decorative sword.

BIBLIOGRAPHY

"America's Changing Religious Landscape." *Pew Research Center*, May 12, 2015. Accessed June 14, 2017. http://www.pewforum.org/2015/05/12/americas-changing-religious-landscape/.

Aristotle. *Nicomachean Ethics*. Translated by H. Rackham. Cambridge: Harvard University Press, 2015.

Bly, Robert. *Iron John: Men and Masculinity*. London: Rider, 2001.

———. *The Sibling Society*. New York: Addison-Wesley, 1996.

Capon, Robert Farrar. *Kingdom, Grace, Judgment: Paradox, Outrage, and Vindication in the Parables of Jesus*. Grand Rapids: Eerdmans, 2002.

Chesterton, G. K. *The Essential Gilbert K. Chesterton*. Vol. 1, *Orthodoxy, Heretics, What's Wrong with the World*. Radford: Wilder, 2007.

———. *Heretics*. Lanham: Dancing Unicorn Books, 2016.

Cicero, Marcus Tullius. *How to Grow Old: Ancient Wisdom for the Second Half of Life*. Translated by Philip Freeman. Princeton: Princeton University Press, 2016.

Forde, Gerhard O. *A More Radical Gospel: Essays on Eschatology, Authority, Atonement, and Ecumenism*. Grand Rapids: Eerdmans, 2004.

French, David. "Male Physical Decline: Masculinity Is Threatened." *National Review*, August 16, 2016. Accessed June 14, 2017. http://www.nationalreview.com/article/439040/male-physical-decline-masculinity-threatened.

Gallagher, Robert P. "National Survey of College Counseling Center Directors." *The International Association of Counseling Services*. Accessed June 14, 2017. http://d-scholarship.pitt.edu/28176/1/Survey_2013_4-yr._Directors_%28Final%29.pdf.

Glyer, Diana Pavlac. "Creative Opposition: If You Want to Be like Lewis, You Need More Tolkien in Your Life." Paper presented at Pacifica Christian High School's C. S. Lewis Symposium, "Education of the

Soul," Newport Beach, CA, October 2–3, 2015. https://www.youtube .com/watch?v=zPc3HfENHYg.

Keith, Scott Leonard. *Being Dad: Father as a Picture of God's Grace*. Irvine: NRP Books, 2015.

Knight, Raymond A., and Robert A. Prentky. "The Developmental Antecedents and Adult Adaptations of Rapist Subtypes." *Criminal Justice and Behavior* 14, no. 4 (1987): 403–26.

Kolb, Robert, and Timothy J. Wengert, eds. *The Book of Concord: The Confessions of the Evangelical Lutheran Church*. Minneapolis: Fortress Press, 2000.

Lewis, C. S. *An Experiment in Criticism*. New York: HarperOne, 2014.

———. *The Four Loves*. San Francisco: HarperOne, 2017.

———. *Surprised by Joy: The Shape of My Early Life*. New York: HarperOne, 2017.

Low, Chris. "Tennessee Volunteers Head Coaches Address Questions over Title IX Lawsuit, Sexual Assault Complaints." *espnW*, February 23, 2016. http://www.espn.com/espnw/sports/article/14829201/ tennessee-volunteers-head-coaches-address-questions-title-ix -lawsuit-sexual-assault-complaints.

Low, Robbie. "The Truth about Men and Church." *Touchstone*, June 2003. http://www.touchstonemag.com/archives/article.php?id=16 -05-024-v.

Luther, Martin, and Harold J. Grimm. *Christian Liberty*. Philadelphia: Fortress Press, 1957.

Luther, Martin, and Ewald Martin Plass. *What Luther Says: An Anthology*. Saint Louis: Concordia, 1972.

Lutheran Church–Missouri Synod. *Lutheran Service Book*. Saint Louis: Concordia, 2006.

"Luther at the Imperial Diet of Worms (1521)." *Luther.de*. Last modified March 10, 2003. http://www.luther.de/en/worms.html.

McGrath, Alister E. *C. S. Lewis—a Life: Eccentric Genius, Reluctant Prophet*. Rearsby, Leicester: W. F. Howes, 2014.

Mitscherlich, Alexander. *Society without Father*. Berlin: Schocken, 1970.

Murrow, Edward R., and Fred W. Friendly. *See It Now*. Television documentary series. Presented by Edward R. Murrow. CBS, March 9, 1954.

Mytting, Lars. *Norwegian Wood: Chopping, Stacking, and Drying Wood the Scandinavian Way*. London: MacLehose, 2015.

Nestingen, James. "Speech—to WordAlone National Gathering." *WordAlone*, March 200, Accessed June 14, 2017. http://wordalone.org/ docs/wa-nestingen-speech-2000.shtml.

Nestingen, James Arne, Gerhard O. Forde, and Corinne Bruning. *Free to Be: A Handbook to Luther's Small Catechism (Student Book)*. Minneapolis: Augsburg, 1975.

Padilla-Walker, Laura M., and Larry J. Nelson. "Black Hawk Down? Establishing Helicopter Parenting as a Distinct Construct from Other Forms of Parental Control during Emerging Adulthood." *Journal of Adolescence* 35, no. 5 (2012): 1177–90. doi: 10.1016/j.adolescence.2012.03.007.

"Public Agenda Foundation Poll: All Work and No Play? What Kids and Parents Really Want from Out-of-School Time." *Roper Center for Public Opinion Research*. Accessed June 14, 2017. https://ropercenter.cornell.edu/CFIDE/cf/action/catalog/abstract.cfm?type=&start=&id=&archno=USPAF2004-TIME&abstract=.

Rollins, Henry. "Iron and the Soul." *Oldtime Strongman*. Accessed June 14, 2017. http://www.oldtimestrongman.com/strength-articles/iron-henry-rollins.

Rowe, Mike. "Don't Follow Your Passion." YouTube video, 5:18. Last modified June 6, 2016. https://www.youtube.com/watch?v=CVEuPmVAb8o.

Sanders, Ryan. "The Father Absence Crisis in America." *National Fatherhood Initiative*, November 12, 2013. Accessed June 14, 2017. http://www.fatherhood.org/the-father-absence-crisis-in-america.

Shakespeare, William. *Henry V*. Edited by Gary Taylor. Oxford: Oxford University Press, 2008.

Veith, Gene Edward. *God at Work: Your Christian Vocation in All of Life*. Wheaton: Crossway Books, 2011.

Walther, C. F. W., Christian C. Tiews, Charles P. Schaum, John P. Hellwege, and Thomas Manteufel. *Law & Gospel: How to Read and Apply the Bible*. St. Louis: Concordia, 2010.

Wordsworth, William. *The Poetical Works of William Wordsworth/The Excursion. The Recluse. P. 1, Book 1*. Oxford: Clarendon Press, 1972.

Zaleski, Philip, and Carol Zaleski. *The Fellowship: The Literary Lives of the Inklings: J. R. R. Tolkien, C. S. Lewis, Owen Barfield, Charles Williams*. New York: Farrar, Straus and Giroux, 2015.

CPSIA information can be obtained
at www.ICGtesting.com
Printed in the USA
FSHW02n0225070918
51882FS